Say and Sing

*Over 200 rhymes and songs
to use with under-5s*

Compiled by
Maggie Barfield

SAY AND SING

© Scripture Union 2006

First published, in this compilation 2006

ISBN   1 84427 245 1
ISBN   978 1 84427 245 7

Scripture Union, 207–209 Queensway, Bletchley, Milton Keynes, MK2 2EB, UK
Email: info@scriptureunion.org.uk
Website: www.scriptureunion.org.uk

Scripture Union Australia, Locked Bag 2, Central Coast Business Centre, NSW 2252, Australia
Website: www.scriptureunion.org.au

Scripture Union USA, PO Box 987, Valley Forge, PA 19482, USA

Scripture quotations are from the Contemporary English Version © American Bible Society 1991, 1992, 1995. Anglicisations © British and Foreign Bible Society 1997, published in the UK by HarperCollinsPublishers. Used by permission.

British Library Cataloguing-in-Publication Data.
A catalogue record of this book is available from the British Library.

Printed and bound by Henry Ling, Dorchester

Cover design: Mark Carpenter Design Consultants

Internal design: John Ball, Creative Pages, www.creativepages.co.uk

Tiddlywinks series editor and compiler: Maggie Barfield

Tiddly characters created by Mark Carpenter

Freelance project manager: Louise Titley, In Edition

Acknowledgements

The items in this book have appeared previously in Scripture Union resources for children in their early years, including *SALT 3 to 4+*, *Bubbles for Leaders*, *Let's Join in!* and *Let's Praise and Pray*. Out of print publications are shown as 'op'.

Thank you to all the freelance writers who have contributed in this way.

Every effort has been made to attribute items correctly, but I apologise to any author whose work has not been properly credited. Please inform the publisher and this will be rectified in any future editions of *Tiddlywinks: Say and Sing*.
Maggie Barfield

Scripture Union is an international charity working with churches in more than 130 countries, providing resources to bring the good news of Jesus Christ to children, young people and families and to encourage them to develop spiritually through the Bible and prayer.

As well as our network of volunteers, staff and associates who run holidays, church-based events and school Christian groups, we produce a wide range of publications and support those who use our resources through training programmes.

Contents

Welcome to *Tiddlywinks: Say and Sing*

Shout praises to the LORD!
Our God is kind,
and it is right and good
to sing praises to him.

Celebrate and sing!
Play your harps for the LORD our God.

The LORD is pleased only
with those who worship him
and trust his love.

Everyone…
come and praise the LORD your God!

Psalm 147:1,7,11,12

Why use rhymes and songs?

Rhymes and songs can introduce, tell or reinforce a theme, story or Bible truth. They can be a way to remember information or a Bible verse, prompt discussion and stimulate interest and response.

Speaking, singing, chanting, actions, dancing, shouting – all these can give us a shared experience and an opportunity for shared pleasure.

Rhymes and songs are effective learning experiences, encourage social development, involve everyone in a group together, and yet enable everyone to participate and develop at their own level and at their own pace.

How to use *Tiddlywinks: Say and Sing*

Suggested actions or sounds are indicated in brackets and italics: *(Wave your hands.)*
Lines or verses for all to respond or join in are in bold type: **God is great!** Or italics: *God is great!*

 the name of the writer or where this has appeared in print

 Bible reference

 you can sing this rhyme to a well-known melody

 ideas for using this item with your children's group

Where to find the tunes

Traditional English folk song tunes, such as 'Bobby Shaftoe', can be found in books of folk music, or by putting the title of the song into an Internet search engine, such as *Google*.

Many nursery tunes can be found in *This Little Puffin…*, Elizabeth Matterson, Puffin Books. This compilation of old and newer pre-school songs is a much used book in many early years groups.

In the UK, Early Learning Centre shops and mail order offer tapes and books of traditional and more modern children's songs and rhymes.

Use the knowledge of others in your church: early years teachers may know songs and older members of the congregation may have a store of song memories you can draw on.

Remember, you can always make up a simple tune yourself or simply speak the words with a strong rhythmic lilt.

By the way, there is no need to tell the children which tune you are using: simply sing the new words to the existing music.

God's big book

What's in a book?

What's in a book? *(Hands together, then open as if opening a book.)*
What's in a book?
There are pictures that we like to see, *(Draw a frame in the air.)*
And lots and lots of words to read, *(Squiggle with fingers as if writing.)*
In stories there for you and me, *(Wave to someone else and then point to self.)*
All in a book. *(Hands together, then open.)*

What's in God's book?
What's in God's book?
There are pictures that we like to see,
And lots and lots of words to read,
God's messages to you and me,
All in God's book.

 Marjory Francis

 Psalm 119; 136:1–9

 'Three blind mice'

 Repeat the same actions for both verses.

What's the Bible?

What's the Bible? What's the Bible?
Do you know? Do you know?
It's God's Word to help us,
To teach us and to guide us.
Thank you God, thank you God.

 Elizabeth Whitworth

 2 Timothy 1:1–10; 3:15–17

 'Frère Jacques'

 Use this song as a start to a regular Bible story time.

What is in the Bible?

What is in the Bible? The Bible? The Bible?
What is in the Bible? In God's book?
Words from God to us, words from God to us,
Words from God to us, in God's book.

What is in the Bible? The Bible? The Bible?
What is in the Bible? In God's book?
Good news for everyone, good news for everyone,
Good news for everyone, in God's book.

What is in the Bible? The Bible? The Bible?
What is in the Bible? In God's book?
Stories Jesus told, stories Jesus told,
Stories Jesus told, in God's book.

What is in the Bible? The Bible? The Bible?
What is in the Bible? In God's book?
Letters people wrote, letters people wrote,
Letters people wrote, in God's book.

 Adapted from *Let's Sing and Shout!* Scripture Union 1998 op

 Luke 4:16–21; Matthew 13:53–58; Mark 6:1–6; Luke 10:25–37; 2 Timothy 1:1–10; 3:15–17

 Choose verses that match the type of Bible story you are telling – or find out about the variety of the Bible by singing the whole song. Improvise your own simple tune.

Praise God!

God is great

So great! God is so great!
There's nothing he can't do.
God is so great!

So kind! God is so kind!
He's always there for you.
God is so kind!

 Christine Wright

 Daniel 6

 A praise shout.

Praise the Lord!

God has been good to us.
Praise the Lord!
He gives us homes where we can live.
Praise the Lord!
He gives us people to care for us.
Praise the Lord!
He helps us when we are afraid.
Praise the Lord!
We'll praise him in the mornings.
Praise the Lord!
We'll praise him in the afternoons.
Praise the Lord!
We'll praise him in the evenings.
Praise the Lord!
We'll praise him all day long.
Praise the Lord!
God is good!
Praise the Lord!
God is great!
Praise the Lord!
God is the best!
Praise the Lord!

 SALT 3 to 4+ January–March 2004

 Nehemiah 12:27–47; Psalm 113:1–3

 Everyone can join in with the repeated refrain, while one person leads strongly and clearly with alternate lines.

God's words

Hear, hear, hear God's words,
Listen to him call,
He loves (*name*) very much,
And he loves us all.

 Rachael Champness

 Matthew 3:1–12; Mark 1:1–8; Luke 3:1–18; John 1:19–28

 'Row, row, row your boat'

 Children love hearing themselves named in this sort of song. Make sure you include everyone, leaders and helpers too! Demonstrate that God loves all of us!

Musical praises

Thank you, God, for music.
God loves to hear our praises!
Thank you, God, for songs.
God loves to hear our praises!
Thank you, God, for voices to sing to you.
God loves to hear our praises!
Thank you, God, for instruments to play.
God loves to hear our praises!
Thank you, God, for listening to us.
God loves to hear our praises!

 Kathryn Bishop

 2 Chronicles 20:1–30; Psalm 150

 Say this prayer before and after a time of musical praise. Enjoy making joyful noises to the Lord!

Talking with God

I love to pray

I love to pray every day,
I love to pray.
I can pray when I walk,
I can pray when I run.
I love to pray every day,
I love to pray.

I can pray with my eyes shut,
Or I can open them wide.
I can fold my hands,
Or hold them high.
I love to pray every day,
I love to pray.

I can pray lying in my bed,
I can pray kneeling on my knees,
I can pray sitting down,
I can pray standing up.
I love to pray every day,
I love to pray.

 SALT 3 to 4+ January–March 2003

 Mark 1:29–39; Matthew 6:5–15; 9:1–8; Luke 5:17–26

 Put the theory of this rhyme into practice and try all the ways listed!

I can talk to God

I can talk to God
With my eyes wide open.
I can talk to God
With them firmly closed.
I can blink, I can wink
With one eye or the other.
God doesn't mind at all.

I can talk to God
With my hands together.
I can talk to God
With hands lifted high.
I can pray all alone,
I can pray with others.
God doesn't mind at all.

I can talk to God
In a quiet whisper.
I can talk out loud
Or in my head.
Whenever I pray,
God always hears me.
God doesn't mind at all.

 Margaret Spivey

 Matthew 6:5–15; Luke 11:2–4

 Use this rhyme to help children realise that talking to God is more important than the *way* in which we do it.

Every minute…

Every minute, every hour, every day,
We can praise our Father God in any way.
We can praise him with a whisper,
We can praise him with a shout,
We can praise him with a clap, clap, clap,
Or stamp our feet about,
Wave our arms up in the air,
Shout, 'Thank you, God, for the fun we share.'
Let's clap again and turn around.
God likes to hear a joyful sound.
We can always find time to say,
'Thank you, God, for each new day!'

 Sheila Clift

 Psalm 113:1–3; Mark 1:2–39

 This rhyme about praying includes short prayers within it. Pray as well as talking about praying!

Talking with God

Talking to God

It doesn't take long to say 'thank you'.
It doesn't take long to say 'please'.
It doesn't take long to say 'sorry',
Or other short prayers like these.
And when God says that he loves me,
And asks me to be his friend,
I know that he means for ever,
'Cos his love will never end.

 Margaret Spivey

 Matthew 6:5–15; Luke 11:2–4

 Prayer is a two-way process. God loves to hear us talk to him – and he talks to us too.

Time to pray

Boys and girls, it's time to pray,
God takes care of us every day.
God is with us, he's always there,
God loves and helps us, he always cares,
He took care of Joseph,
He takes care of me.
So now we'll say, 'Thank you, God,'
One, two, three!
(*Stop, raise hands and shout, 'Thank you God!'*)

 Margaret Spivey

 Genesis 42 – 45

 'Boys and girls come out to play'

 This song was originally written about Joseph but there are many other Bible characters whose names could be put into line 5 instead.

When can we pray?

We can pray all the time and you always say
You will answer the prayers that we pray.

We can pray in the morning when we wake up.
(*Stretch and pretend to wake up.*)
'Dear God, be with us in our day.'

We can pray in the daytime when we're busy at home.
(*Pretend to be helping with household tasks or playing.*)
'Dear God, please help us when we play.'

We can pray at meal times when we're eating our food.
(*Mime eating.*)
'Dear God, thank you for our food.'

We can pray at night time when we're going to bed.
(*Curl up and pretend to go to sleep.*)
'Jesus, thank you for being our friend.'

We can pray all the time and you always say
You will answer the prayers that we pray.

 Bubbles for Leaders April–June 2006

 1 Samuel 1:9–20; Ephesians 6:18

 Think about times when you can pray – and then pray the prayer.

Time with God

God talks

Do you know God talks to you,
God talks to you, God talks to you?
Do you know God talks to you?
Just listen every day.

Yes, I know God talks to me,
God talks to me, God talks to me.
Yes, I know God talks to me.
I'll listen every day.

Do you know God speaks to you,
God speaks to you, God speaks to you?
Do you know God speaks to you?
He says he loves you so.

Yes, I know God speaks to me,
God speaks to me, God speaks to me.
Yes, I know God speaks to me.
He says he loves me so.

 Ruth Dell

 Judges 7:1–22

 'Do you know the muffin man?'

 Divide into two groups, each with a leader, and sing alternate verses to each other as questions and answers. Swap roles and repeat.

Me and you, God

Just me and you, God, just me and you,
You hear what I say, God, you know what I do.
You know who I am, God, you made me this way,
You know what I'm like, God. You love me – hooray!

 Margaret Spivey

 Psalm 139; Luke 18:9–17

 Children need to know and experience God's unconditional love for them.

Close to God

We're happy when we're close to God,
Since that's where we belong.
But sometimes we go far from God,
And everything feels wrong.

But God will draw us back to him,
His love is sure and strong.
We're happy when we're close to God,
And that's where we belong.

 Mary Houlgate

 Genesis 3

 Young children have limited understanding of right and wrong, so these words focus on having a renewed relationship with God.

God and us

Safe with God

God you are our strong place,
(Make a tower with arms above your head.)
You always keep us safe when things are going wrong.
(Hug arms around yourself.)
So we won't be afraid
(Shake head and lift index finger.)
Even when the waters rush and foam and the big, big waves splash the mountains,
(Wave arms in big sweeps, then clap hands together.)
We will thank you, because you care for us and will always help.
(Point upwards and point to each other.)
Amen.
(Fold hands and sit with head bowed.)

 Elizabeth Whitworth

 Psalm 46

We are safe

Father God is near,
We are safe,
Watching all his lambs,
We are safe.
He takes away our fear,
We are safe,
Safe in our
Father's hands.

 SALT 3 to 4+ July–September 2004

 Psalm 23

 'Kumbaya'

 The lilting tune and repeated assurance of this song gives young children a sense of security and comfort with God.

God's big family

Brothers, sisters, friends are we,
Singing together, merrily.
We're as happy as can be,
All in God's big family.

Brothers, sisters, friends are we,
Clapping together, merrily.
We're as happy as can be,
All in God's big family.

Brothers, sisters, friends are we,
Praising together, merrily.
We're as happy as can be,
All in God's big family.

Brothers, sisters, friends are we,
Loving together, merrily.
We're as happy as can be,
All in God's big family.

Brothers, sisters, friends are we,
Reading our Bibles, merrily.
We're as happy as can be,
All in God's big family.

 Margaret Spivey

 Genesis 42 – 45; Galatians 3:28,29

 'Horsey, horsey, don't you stop'

 Ask the children for ideas and see how many verses you can write for this song.

God and us

God's family

Tell me, tell me, please can you tell me,
How does God's family grow?

When people want to be God's friends,
Then that's how God's family grows,
That's how God's family grows.

 Bubbles for Leaders January–March 2005

 Mark 4:26–29

 'Mary, Mary quite contrary'

 Form two groups (each with an adult) so the children can ask and answer the question. All sing the last line. Swap roles and repeat.

Family and friends

Thank you for my family.
Thank you, God, that they love me.
Thanks for all they tell of you,
What you say and what you do.
Thank you for my family.
Thank you, God, that they love me.

Thank you, God, for friends as well.
They have lots of tales to tell –
Stories when I learn of you
What you say and what you do.
Thank you, God, for friends as well.
They have lots of tales to tell.

 Priscilla Trood

 Luke 24:13–35; Mark 16:12,13; 2 Timothy 1:2–8

 'Twinkle, twinkle little star'

God's way

I will praise God for his Word, yes I will!
I will praise God for his Word, yes I will!
In my work and in my play,
In the night and in the day,
I will praise God for his Word, yes I will!

God will help me do things his way, yes he will!
God will help me do things his way, yes he will!
In my work and in my play,
In the night and in the day,
God will help me do things his way, yes he will!

 Christine Orme

 Psalm 119:161,162,168

 'If you're happy and you know it'

 We do not have to try and live God's way on our own: God will help and guide us, all the time.

Friends with God

Friends of God

When you show your love,
When I show my love,
When you and I both show our love,
Then we are friends of God.

When you talk to God,
When I talk to God,
When you and I both talk to him,
Then we are friends of God.

When you believe in God,
When I believe in God,
When you and I both believe in him,
Then we are friends of God.

You say, 'Thank you, God',
I say, 'Thank you, God',
When you and I say thanks to him,
Then we are friends of God.

 Let's Join in! Scripture Union 1990 op

 Mark 10:17–27; Matthew 19:16–30; Luke 18:18–30

 Young children need readily understood examples of what it means to say they are friends of God.

God loves us all

Some people, they are rather short and others they are tall.
Some people's ears are very big and others' very small.
Some people have a lot of hair and some have none at all.
But it really doesn't matter 'cos God loves us all!

Some people have brown faces and some faces are white.
Some people are quite heavy and some are very light.
Some people they are very brave and some get scared at night!
But God loves us anyway – so everything's all right!

Some people live in cold lands and others live in hot.
Some people have a little and others have a lot.
And some need specs and hearing-aids and some people do not.
But God loves all of us the same, no matter what!

 Christine Orme

 Acts 10

God looks after us

God looks after me, *(Point at self.)*
God looks after you, *(Point towards someone else.)*
Wherever we go, *(Walk on the spot.)*
Whatever we do, *('Roll' hands over and over.)*
God looks after us. *(Thumbs up.)*

 Christine Wright

 Acts 12:4–17

 'The farmer's in his den'

Friends with God

Everywhere!

God looks after us everywhere,
He watches us here,
He watches us there,
God looks after us everywhere.

God looks after me everywhere,
He watches me here,
He watches me there,
God looks after me everywhere.

 Christine Wright

 Psalm 139; Acts 12:4–17

 Repeat, inserting the names of the children in your group (instead of 'me'), until everyone has had the prayer said for them.

Trust God!

Praise the Lord, pray in his name,
Trust God and his mighty power!
Tell everyone what he has done! Sing praises to the Lord!
Trust God and his mighty power!
God will never forget his promises,
Trust God and his mighty power!
God sent Joseph, a slave into Egypt until he had finished testing him,
Trust God and his mighty power!
Then the king of Egypt set Joseph free and put him in charge of everything he owned.
Trust God and his mighty power!
God taught the leaders to be wise.
Trust God and his mighty power!
Shout praises to the Lord!
Trust God and his mighty power!
Trust God and his mighty power!

 Alison Gidney

 Psalm 105

 Say this responsive rhyme dramatically, to demonstrate the mighty power of God!

One, two, three

Step one, two, three and follow me,
Step one, two, three, step quietly. *(Whisper.)*
Step one, two, three and touch your nose,
Step one, two, three and touch your toes.
Step one, two, three and crouch down small,
Step one, two, three and stand up tall.
Step one, two, three and clap for joy,
God loves every girl and boy.

 Sheila Clift

 Genesis 12:1–9

Being 'me'

I'm growing!

Now I am one
(Hold up one finger.)
I think it is fun
To shake a rattle
(Mime.)
And sleep in the sun.
(Fold hands under head.)

Now I am two
(Hold two fingers.)
I think it is cool
To splash in the bath
(Mime.)
And play 'Peek-a-boo'.
(Demonstrate.)

Now I am three
(Three fingers.)
As you can see,
I can run, walk and play –
(Pump arms and legs.)
It's fun being me!
(Point to self.)

Now I am four
(Four fingers.)
I can do much more.
I skip, hop and jump
(Jump on the spot.)
And roll on the floor.
(Roll arms.)

Now I am five
(Five fingers.)
I've really arrived.
I'm learning so fast,
(Roll arms quickly.)
And glad I'm alive!
(Raise arms in the air.)

 Christine Wright

 Matthew 25:1–13

 Young children enjoy reviewing how much they have changed, grown and developed.

Mirror-me!

When I look in the mirror, what do you think I see?
I see someone God cares for, looking back at me.
When I look in the mirror, I'm sure as I can be.
That God, who loves everyone, is looking after me.

 Christine Wright

 Acts 12:4–17

 As children develop a sense of 'self', they often spend time staring in a mirror, getting used to 'being me'. Provide as many mirrors as you can for children to use, casually, during your time together. When you notice a child playing with the mirror, join them and ask who they are looking at. Comment that God sees us – without a mirror – all the time! Chat together about how good it feels to know that God is always looking after us.

Jesus and us

Jesus wants to be our friend

All the people in the world –
Jesus wants to be your friend!
All the people in *(your country)* –
Jesus wants to be your friend!
All the people in *(your town)* –
Jesus wants to be your friend!
All the people in *(name of your church)* –
Jesus wants to be your friend!
All the people in *(name of your group)* –
Jesus wants to be your friend!

Thank you, Jesus, thank you, Jesus,
That you want to be our friend!

 Alison Hulse

 Mark 10:17–27; Matthew 19:16–30; Luke 18:18–30

 Customise this rhyme to suit your own situation. Encourage everyone to join in with: 'Jesus wants to be your friend!' Try repeating the rhyme and, this time, clap four beats as you say the responsive line. You might like to ask individual children, 'Does Jesus want to be your friend?'

Loved by Jesus

Dear Jesus,
We are happy that you love us all,
Whether we're big or whether we're small,
Whether we're up or whether we're down,
If we're in our house, or in the village or town,
If we walk to the shops, if we go in the car,
If we climb up trees or journey far,
Wherever we go and whatever we do,
Thank you Jesus, that we're loved by you.

 Alison Irving

 Psalm 139; Luke 19:1–10

 Extend the rhyme by adding more places and times when we can be sure that Jesus loves us.

A special friend

Thank you, God, that we can know Jesus.
Jesus is our special friend.
Thank you that we can learn about Jesus.
Jesus is our special friend.
Thank you for the way Jesus loves us.
Jesus is our special friend.
Help us to follow him and be his friend.
Jesus is our special friend.

 SALT 3 to 4+ October–December 2003

 John 1:35–51

 Being a friend of Jesus is about more than knowing Bible stories.

Jesus and us

Who will come and help?

When I'm feeling lonely,
When I'm feeling lonely,
When I'm feeling lonely,
Who will come and help?
Who will come and help?
Who will come and help?
My friend will come and help me, (x3)
And make me smile again.

When I'm sad or crying,
When I'm sad or crying,
When I'm sad or crying,
Who will come and help?
Who will come and help?
Who will come and help?
My friend will come and help me, (x3)
And make me smile again.

When I'm feeling lonely,
When I'm feeling lonely,
When I'm feeling lonely,
Who will come and help?
Who will come and help?
Who will come and help?
Jesus will come and help me, (x3)
And make me smile again.

When I'm sad or crying,
When I'm sad or crying,
When I'm sad or crying,
Who will come and help?
Who will come and help?
Who will come and help?
Jesus will come and help me, (x3)
And make me smile again.

 Christine Wright

 Matthew 15:21–28; Mark 7:24–30; Luke 18:15–17;
Revelation 21:1–4

 'The bear went over the mountain'

 Discuss different reasons for needing help. Then sing some of the
following verses or others of your own:

When I'm hurt or poorly...

When I'm hungry or thirsty...

When I'm tired and sleepy...

All-over thanks!

Thank God with my fingers, *(Wiggle your fingers.)*
Thank God with my toes, *(Wiggle your toes.)*
Thank God with my eyes and mouth,
(Blink eyes and wiggle mouths.)
Thank God with my nose. *(Wiggle nose.)*
Thank God every *Easter*,
Thank God every day,
Thank God now for Jesus
And shout out loud: Hooray!

 Ali Matchett

 Mark 16:9–20; Matthew 28:9,10,16–20; John 20:11–18;
Luke 24:13–53; John 20:19–23; Acts 1:6–11

 What actions would the children suggest for the second part of the
prayer? Experiment and then repeat the whole prayer. Adapt the
fifth line for other times or festivals.

Jesus helps

Who can help us every day?
Jesus can, Jesus can!
He can help us every day!
Thank you, thank you Jesus!

 Geraldine Witcher

 Matthew 8:5–13; Luke 7:1–10; John 4:43–54

Jesus and us

Jesus the shepherd

Jesus the shepherd will guide his sheep,
And lead them to all the safe places.
He loves one and all, the big and the small,
He knows all their names and their faces.

Jesus the shepherd takes care of his sheep,
And leads them away from all danger.
The sheep know his voice, they hear and rejoice,
Because he's their friend, not a stranger.

Jesus the shepherd loves all of his sheep,
He leads them to tasty green grasses.
He keeps them in sight, they're safe day and night,
He watches until danger passes.

 Priscilla Trood

 John 10:1–21

 'Little Bo Peep'

 The gentle rhythm and reassuring words of this rhyme will help give young children a sense of belonging, security and safety with Jesus.

Safe with Jesus

Jesus says, 'I'm always near,
Even when you're full of fear.
I will keep you safe from harm
So be at peace, feel safe and calm.'

 Priscilla Trood

 John 10:1–21

 This short rhyme could be used to end your session each time you meet.

When we're sorry

I'm glad I belong to Jesus.
(Point to self.)
I'm glad you belong too!
(Point to others.)
I'm glad that, when we're sorry,
(Place hands together.)
He forgives both me and you.
(Clap.)

 Margaret Spivey

 Luke 18:9–14

 Young children are only just beginning to understand the meaning of right and wrong so this rhyme is deliberately low-key.

Happy with God

Clap and tap and nod

Thank you for my hands, which can clap, clap, clap.
Thank you for my feet, which can tap, tap, tap.
Thank you for my head, which can nod, nod, nod.
All these were given me by God, God, God.

 Priscilla Trood

 John 11:1–44

 The actions for this rhyme speak for themselves – but why not make up more verses and devise your own movements to go with them?

We can choose

We cannot choose to be big,
(Stretch arms and legs out to the side.)
We cannot choose to be small,
(Scrunch into a small shape.)
We cannot choose to be little,
(Crouch down low.)
We cannot choose to be tall,
(Stretch up on tiptoes.)

But there's one thing God helps us to choose –
He helps us to choose what is right.
(Nod.)
We can choose to do things God's way,
We can choose to do what is right.
(Thumbs up.)

 SALT 3 to 4+ July–September 2004

 1 Samuel 24; 1 Kings 3; 2 Chronicles 1:1–13

God looks after me

God is with me when I travel,
I travel, I travel,
God is with me when I travel,
God knows where I am.
(Join hands and move round in a line.)

God is with me when I'm playing,
I'm playing, I'm playing,

God is with me when I'm playing,
God looks after me.
(Mime playing with a favourite toy: guess what each other is doing.)

God is with me when I'm sleeping,
I'm sleeping, I'm sleeping,
God is with me when I'm sleeping,
God looks after me.
(Lean your head on your hands and whisper.)

God says he will be with me,
Be with me, be with me,
God says he will be with me,
I know that he's here.
(Thumbs up.)

 Pam Priestley

 Genesis 13; Psalm 139

 'Poor Mary sits a-weeping'

 Sing the whole song to think about God being with us all the time and everywhere. Or choose one or two verses to focus on particular times and occasions.

God's wonderful world

God's wonderful world

This is God's wonderful world.
(*Make big circle with hands.*)

Here is the sun, shining so bright
That God put in his wonderful world.

Here are the silvery moon and stars,
Here is the sun, shining so bright
That God put in his wonderful world.

Here is the sea with splashing waves,
Here are the silvery moon and stars,
Here is the sun, shining so bright
That God put in his wonderful world.

Here are creatures which live in the sea,
Here is the sea with splashing waves,
Here are the silvery moon and stars,
Here is the sun, shining so bright
That God put in his wonderful world.

Here is the sky, way up high,
Here are creatures which live in the sea,
Here is the sea with splashing waves,
Here are the silvery moon and stars,
Here is the sun, shining so bright
That God put in his wonderful world.

Here are birds which fly in the sky,
Here is the sky, way up high,
Here are creatures which live in the sea,
Here is the sea with splashing waves,
Here are the silvery moon and stars,
Here is the sun, shining so bright
That God put in his wonderful world.

Here is the land with plants and trees,
Here are birds which fly in the sky,
Here is the sky, way up high,
Here are creatures which live in the sea,
Here is the sea with splashing waves,
Here are the silvery moon and stars,
Here is the sun, shining so bright
That God put in his wonderful world.

Here are the rain clouds that water the land,
Here is the land with plants and trees,
Here are birds which fly in the sky,
Here is the sky, way up high,
Here are creatures which live in the sea,
Here is the sea with splashing waves,
Here are the silvery moon and stars,
Here is the sun, shining so bright
That God put in his wonderful world.

Here are animals, big and small,
Here are the rain clouds that water the land,
Here is the land with plants and trees,
Here are birds which fly in the sky,
Here is the sky, way up high,
Here are creatures which live in the sea,
Here is the sea with splashing waves,
Here are the silvery moon and stars,
Here is the sun, shining so bright
That God put in his wonderful world.

And here are some people God made,
Here are animals, big and small,
Here are the rain clouds that water the land,
Here is the land with plants and trees,
Here are birds which fly in the sky,
Here is the sky, way up high,
Here are creatures which live in the sea,
Here is the sea with splashing waves,
Here are the silvery moon and stars,
Here is the sun, shining so bright
That God put in his wonderful world.

 Kathleen Crawford

 Psalm 104; Genesis 1 – 2:4

 After each verse, everyone can join in the words, 'That God put in his wonderful world' and make a big circle in the air with their hands. Practise this a few times first.

You may need to allow extra time for repetition if the children are enjoying this activity.

God the maker

What do they wear?

What do the animals and the fish wear?
What clothes clothe the birds in the sky?
Who gave us skin and nails and hair?
Who put the wings on the fly?

Animals wear soft fur,
(*Stroking action.*)
Soft fur, soft fur,
(*Stroking.*)
Animals wear soft fur,
(*Stroking.*)
To keep them dry.

What do the animals and the fish wear?
What clothes clothe the birds in the sky?
Who gave us skin and nails and hair?
Who put the wings on the fly?

Fish wear slippery scales,
(*Wave motion with hand.*)
Slippery scales, slippery scales,
(*Wave.*)
Fish wear slippery scales,
(*Wave.*)
As they swim by.

What do the animals and the fish wear?
What clothes clothe the birds in the sky?
Who gave us skin and nails and hair?
Who put the wings on the fly?

Birds wear bright feathers,
(*Arms up and down like wings.*)
Bright feathers, bright feathers,
(*Up and down.*)
Birds wear bright feathers,
(*Up and down.*)
Up in the sky.

What do the animals and the fish wear?
What clothes clothe the birds in the sky?
Who gave us skin and nails and hair?
Who put the wings on the fly?

God gave the animals fur to wear,
(*Stroking.*)
God gave the fish their scales,
(*Wave.*)
God put the feathers on the bright birds,
(*Up and down.*)
He made good things for you and I.
(*Point to one another.*)

 Alison Irving

 Genesis 2:1–4; Psalm 147; Matthew 6:25–30, 10:29–31; Luke 12:6–7

 Younger children will need reminders as the lines of each verse get longer but keep this light-hearted and enjoy the final verse with all the answers!

God made...

God made lions, God made rats,
God made snakes and God made cats.
God made chicks, God made frogs,
God made birds and God made dogs.
God made fruit, God made flowers,
God made sunshine, God made showers,
God made grass, God made trees,
God made you and God made me!

 SALT 3 to 4+ July–September 2002

 Genesis 1

 What else did God make? Everything you can name – and everything else too!

God the maker

Who made them?

Who made the stars?
Father God.
Who made the sun?
Father God
Who made the moon?
Father God.
Thank you Father God.

Geraldine Witcher

Genesis 1:14–19; Psalm 104

Who is it?

Who put the gold in 'golden'?
Who put the bright sun in the sky?
Who is so special that he loves us?
He's like treasure to you and I.

Who put the rain in rainbow?
Who made wind on a windy day?
God is the one who loves us.
'Thank you God,' the children say.

Who made the stars in the night-time?
Who put the fish in the sea?
Who is so very glad he knows us?
Because he loves us, you and me!

Alison Irving

Matthew 13:44–46; Psalm 104; Genesis 1 – 2:4

Who made it?

I think about the world so great,
With sea and seaside, land and light.
Tell me who made the world I see –
Father God – and he made me!

I think about the sky above,
Bright by day and dark by night.
Tell me who made the sky I see –
Father God – and he made me!

I think about the graceful trees,
The grass and fruits and flowers and seeds.
Tell me who made the world I see –
Father God – and he made me!

I think about the golden sun,
The silver stars and glowing moon.
Tell me who made the light I see –
Father God – and he made me!

Bubbles for Leaders September–December 2004

Genesis 1; Psalm 139

God the maker

Creation

A long time ago,
There was nothing here at all,
God made the world,
And gave it to us all.

He made the day,
He made the night,
Sun, moon and stars,
To give us light.

The ground where we walk,
The sea where we swim,
The trees that we climb,
Are a gift from him.

The fish in the sea,
The birds in the air,
He made all the animals,
For everyone to share.

And God was very pleased,
With all that he could see,
And so he made some people,
Just like you and me.

 SALT 3 to 4+ July–September 2002

 Genesis 1

 God made everything – and it can be good to be reminded that 'everything' includes us!

Little things

Let's pretend to be
Tiny things to see.
A snail crawling over a stone, then hiding inside his home.
A beautiful butterfly
Flying lightly through the sky.
A tiny seed that grows and grows
Into an apple tree or a rose.
Let's pretend to be
Tiny things to see.
Thank you, God, for making tiny things.

 SALT 3 to 4+ July–September 2002

 Genesis 1; Matthew 13:31,32; Mark 4:30–32; Luke 13:18–21

 This rhyme keys into a young child's fascination with tiny objects and creatures.

Praise God, everyone!

Praise God, praise God, everyone,
(Clap.)
Praise our God the mighty one.
(Clap.)
He loves me and he loves you.
(Point to yourself, then others.)
He wants us to love him too.
(Hold hands palms upward.)
Praise God, praise God, everyone,
(Clap.)
Praise our God the mighty one.
(Clap.)

 SALT 3 to 4+ July–September 2001

 Luke 9:1–6; Matthew 10:5–15; Mark 6:7–13; Luke 18:15–17; Matthew 19:13–15; Mark 10:13–16

 'Twinkle, twinkle little star'

God makes people

God made people

Our God made people who could clap and wave,
Clap and wave, clap and wave.
Our God made people who could clap and wave.
God is good.

Our God made people who can speak and think,
Speak and think, speak and think,
Our God made people who can speak and think,
God is good.

Our God made people who can sing and dance,
Sing and dance, sing and dance,
Our God made people who can sing and dance,
God is good.

Our God made people who can paint and draw,
Paint and draw, paint and draw,
Our God made people who can paint and draw,
God is good.

Our God made people who can smile and laugh,
Smile and laugh, smile and laugh,
Our God made people who can smile and laugh,
God is good.

Our God made people who can pray and praise,
Pray and praise, pray and praise,
Our God made people who can pray and praise,
God is good.

Our God made people who can care for others,
Care for others, care for others,
Our God made people who can care for others,
God is good.

Our God made people who can care for his world,
Care for his world, care for his world,
Our God made people who can care for his world,
God is good.

 Kathleen Crawford

 Genesis 2:5–25; 1 Corinthians 12:12–31

 'The wheels on the bus'

 This song can grow to be as long as your imaginations and endurance allow!

Adam and Eve

Adam and Eve were the very first family,
The first two people that God ever made.
Adam and Eve, one man, one woman –
The very first family that God ever made.

Adam and Eve had a new baby boy,
The first baby boy that ever was made.
Adam and Eve and Cain, their baby –
The very first family that God ever made.

Adam and Eve had another small baby,
The first baby brother that ever was made.
Adam and Eve and Cain and Abel –
The very first family that God ever made.

 Christine Wright

 Genesis 4:1,2

 Count the members of the family on your finger. Wiggle your index fingers as Adam and Eve, and little fingers as Cain and Abel.

Noah

Noah's boat

Hammer, hammer, hammer, hammer,
Hammer all day, hammer all night.
We have to build a great big boat,
We have to get it right!

Saw, saw, saw, saw,
Saw all day, saw all night.
We have to build a great big boat,
We have to get it right!

Drill, drill, drill, drill,
Drill all day, drill all night.
We have to build a great big boat,
We have to get it right!

Paint, paint, paint, paint,
Paint all day, paint all night.
We have to build a great big boat,
We have to get it right!

Quick! quick! quick! quick!
Get in the boat, the rain is here!
(Run around or on the spot.)
God told us he'll keep us safe *(Stop.)*
Until the water has gone!

 Elizabeth Whitworth

 Genesis 6 – 7

 This rhyme lends itself to plenty of actions and sound effects!

Safe and dry

Noah and the animals stayed in the boat,
Safe from the water because it could float.
Then the water went down and down,
And they were standing on solid ground,
And a rainbow shone high up above,
To show Noah's family of God's love.
Isn't God great to keep them together,
All safe and dry and out of the weather?

 Elizabeth Whitworth

 Genesis 6 – 9

Thank you for the rainbow

Thank you for the rainbow, Lord,
Thank you for red.
Thank you for the rainbow, Lord,
Thank you for orange.
Thank you for the rainbow, Lord,
Thank you for yellow.
Thank you for the rainbow, Lord,
Thank you for green.
Thank you for the rainbow, Lord,
Thank you for bright blue.
Thank you for the rainbow, Lord,
Thank you for dark blue.
Thank you for the rainbow, Lord,
Thank you for purple.
But most of all, Lord,
Thank you that the rainbow shows
That you remember us!

 Elizabeth Whitworth

 Genesis 8:1 – 9:17

 Repeat the chant and this time change the last word to 'me'.

Noah

In Noah's boat

Noah built a house to float,
Noah built a wooden boat,
Took inside his wife and sons,
Animals and food for everyone.
God shut the door upon them all.
They waited for the rain to fall.

Eight people in the boat
(Hold up eight fingers.)
And it rained all day.
(Wiggle fingers downwards.)
They tossed on the stormy sea –
(Rock from side to side.)
Eight people in the boat
(Hold up eight fingers.)
Who'd heard God say,
(Cup ear.)
'You're safe if you trust in me.'
(Hold out hands, palms up.)

The days went by inside the ark,
Animals and people in the dark.
They felt the waters slosh about,
They wondered when they would get out.
They trusted God it was safe inside.
They could wait till the storms had died.

Eight people…

At last, a day with no more rain,
The water's going down again.
The tossing and the rocking stop,
The boat is on a mountain top.
Open the window to see outside
And wait until the ground has dried.

Eight people…

No more need for a house to float!
No more need for a wooden boat!
Now the earth is safe and dry,
See the rainbow in the sky!
Open the door and feel the sun!
Give praise to God for what he's done!

 Let's Join in! Scripture Union 1990 op

 Genesis 6 – 9

God loved Noah

Noah and his family all loved God,
They listened very carefully and did as God had asked.
Noah built a great big boat,
It was long and tall and very wide.
Their neighbours thought it very odd,
And laughed and laughed and laughed.
BUT who loved Noah?
God loved Noah.
Who loved Noah?
God loved Noah.

 Kathryn Bishop

 Genesis 6:9–22

Two by two

We are marching two by two, hurrah, hurrah,
We are marching two by two, hurrah, hurrah,
We are marching two by two, *Katie and Jason* – God loves you!
And we'll march and sing because God loves us all!

 Bubbles for Leaders January–March 2005

 Genesis 6:9–22

 'The animals went in two by two'

 March around the room together, singing the song. Call out two names in line 3. Repeat until everyone has been named in this way.

Abraham

A new land

God said to Abraham:
'I – I want – I want you –
I want you to –
I want you to go –
I want you to go to – where? **A new land!'**

Abraham said to God:
'Yes – Yes we – Yes we will –
Yes we will go –
Yes we will go to – where? **A new land!'**

Abraham said to Sarah:
'Let's – Let's pack – Let's pack up –
Let's pack up and –
Let's pack up and go to – where? **A new land!'**

Abraham and Sarah talked to their friends and said,
'Come with us –
We'll – We'll have – We'll have a –
We'll have a new –
We'll have a new life in – where? **A new land!'**

Abraham and Sarah trusted God and did as he asked because they knew that,
God's – God's big – God's big plan –
God's big plan would –
God's big plan would start in – where? **A new land!**

So Abraham and Sarah and their friends packed up all their things, waved 'goodbye' and set off to follow God's big plan to – where? **A new land!**

God says to us:
'I – I want – I want you –
I want you to –
I want you to belong –
I want you to belong to – who? **Me!'**

Let's say to God:
'Yes – Yes we – Yes we will –
Yes we will belong –
Yes we will belong to – who? **You!'**

God says to us:
'I – I want – I want you –
I want you to –
I want you to do –
I want you to do – what? **What I ask!'**

Let's say to God:
'Yes – Yes we – Yes we will –
Yes we will do –
Yes we will do – what? **What you ask!'**

God says to us:
'I – I want – I want you –
I want you to –
I want you to – say –
I want you to say – what? **"Yes" to me!'**

Let's say to God:
'Yes – Yes we – Yes we will –
Yes we will say –
Yes we will say – what? **"Yes" to you!'**

 Sheila Clift

 Genesis 12:1–9

 Encourage the children to repeat each phrase in italics, after you, building up the sentences one word at a time. Everyone can shout the words at the end of each verse.

Abraham

Abraham and Sarah

Abraham and Sarah,
Abraham and Sarah,
Abraham and Sarah,
Set off for a new land.

God promised to be with them,
God promised to be with them,
God promised to be with them,
And they believed in him.

They travelled and they travelled,
They travelled and they travelled,
They travelled and they travelled,
To get to the new land.

At last they reached the new land,
At last they reached the new land,
At last they reached the new land,
The land God chose for them.

Now they had a new home,
Now they had a new home,
Now they had a new home,
The home God chose for them.

They knew that God was with them,
They knew that God was with them,
They knew that God was with them,
And they believed in him.

 Let's Join in! Scripture Union 1990 op

 Genesis 12:1 – 13:18

 'Round and round the village'

 Act out Abraham's journey as you sing. You can use the second verse as a chorus to emphasise God's promise to the travellers.

Abram obeys

God came and spoke to Abram one day,
'Now, pack up all your things and move away,
Take your pots and take your pans,
Travel to a far-off land,
Because Canaan is the place for you to stay.'

Abram listened and he trusted God and so
He shouted, 'YES! Our love for God will grow,
When we take our pots and pans,
And go to a far-off land,
And we know that God will help us as we go.'

 Sheila Clift

 Genesis 12:1–9

 'If you're happy and you know it'

Jacob

Jacob lay sleeping

Jacob lay sleeping down on the cold ground;
His pillow was made from a stone.
His friends and his family were far, far away,
He felt sad to be all on his own.

While Jacob was sleeping, God sent him a dream –
A stairway that reached to the sky,
God's servants, the angels, walked up it and down.
To Jacob, God spoke from close by.

'Don't worry, dear Jacob, you're *not* on your own,
I'm your God, and I'm everywhere.
Whatever you do and wherever you go
You'll be safe in my loving care.'

God took care of Jacob; he takes care of me;
He's with *me* wherever I go!
God never forgets me; he's always right there,
He's my friend, and he loves me, I know.

Christine Orme

Genesis 28:10–22

Esau and Jacob

Here is Esau and his twin,
(Hold up thumbs, side by side.)
Jacob is his name.
But these brothers aren't good friends,
(Move thumbs apart.)
Isn't that a shame?

One day, Jacob tricked his brother.
(Wiggle one thumb.)
Esau, he was mad!
(Shake other thumb.)
Jacob ran away from home,
(Hide first thumb, behind back.)
Feeling scared and sad.

Home again came brother Jacob,
(Bring first thumb out again slowly.)
After years away.

But he wondered, 'What will Esau
Think or do or say?'

Esau ran to meet his brother,
(Move thumbs together.)
Jacob bowed down low.
Jacob said, 'I'm sorry, Esau.'
Esau said, 'Hello!'

Esau forgave Jacob,
So the trouble ends,
(Hold thumbs side by side.)
Now the family is happy,
Because the twins are friends.

Let's Join in! Scripture Union 1990 op

Genesis 25:19–34; 27:1–45; 32:1 – 33:17

A finger rhyme.

Joseph

Joseph's brothers

'What shall we do with our stuck-up brother?
What shall we do with our stuck-up brother?
What shall we do with our stuck-up brother?'
Said the sons of Jacob.

'Let's get rid of him forever,
Let's get rid of him forever,
Let's get rid of him forever,'
Said the sons of Jacob.

'Don't kill him, put him in a deep, dark hole,
Don't kill him, put him in a deep, dark hole,
Don't kill him, put him in a deep, dark hole,'
Said Reuben, son of Jacob.

Along came traders on their camels,
Along came traders on their camels,
Along came traders on their camels,
To the sons of Jacob.

'Let's trade Joseph for some silver,
Let's trade Joseph for some silver,
Let's trade Joseph for some silver,'
Said Judah, son of Jacob.

They told lies to their father Jacob,
They told lies to their father Jacob,
They told lies to their father Jacob,
Oh those sons of Jacob!

 Mary Houlgate

 Genesis 37:12–36

 'What shall we do with the drunken sailor?'

 This song tells some of the darker events of Joseph's story. Make sure you use it within the context of God's love and protection for his people and assure young children that there is a happy ending to the story.

God loved Joseph

God loved Joseph,
God loved Joseph,
God helped him,
God helped him,
God was always with him,
God was always with him,
Thank you, God!
Thank you, God!

God loves *Phoebe*,
God loves *Phoebe*,
God helps her,
God helps her.
God is always with her,
God is always with her,
Thank you, God!
Thank you, God!

 Bubbles for Leaders April–June 2005

 Genesis 41 – 47

 'Frère Jacques'

 Once the children understand that God looked after Joseph, talk together about how God also looks after us today. Continue the song, using the names of the children in your group. Pray: 'Thank you, God, that you helped Joseph. Thank you, God, that you help us. Thank you, God, that you are always with us.'

Joseph

God was there!

Joseph's father loved him,
And gave him bright clothes to wear.
Joseph thought, 'I'm special'.
And *God was there!*

Joseph's brothers were angry,
They said 'It's not fair!'
They sent poor Joseph away.
And *God was there!*

Joseph was sad in Egypt.
No one seemed to care.
Everything went wrong for him.
And *God was there!*

The king was very worried.
Everyone was scared.
Joseph told them what to do.
And *God was there!*

Joseph was important now.
He had food to share.
Joseph had a special job.
And *God was there!*

Joseph's brothers came for food.
'Please will you be fair?'
Joseph told them who he was.
And *God was there!*

Joseph hugged his brothers.
His father came to share
In happy times in Egypt.
And *God was there!*

Joseph knew in good and bad
That always, God was there.
When we are sad or happy,
Then *God is there!*

 Alison Dayer

 Genesis 37 – 47

 Say all of the rhyme or choose individual verses to tell certain parts of the Joseph story.

Joseph

God kept Joseph safe with him,
Safe with him, safe with him,
God kept Joseph safe with him,
God took good care of him.

 Bubbles for Leaders April–June 2005

 Genesis 37 – 47

 'Mary had a little lamb'

 Sing this song to accompany any story of Joseph – including the times when he did not seem at all safe!

Moses

Baby Moses

Moses is in danger.
Soldiers here,
March march, march march.
(*Pat hands on legs.*)

Mummy makes a basket
Out of grass,
Swish swish, swish swish.
(*Wave hands to look like long grass.*)

Moses in the basket,
Sleeps inside,
Rock rock, rock rock.
(*Rock baby in arms.*)

Princess in the water,
Hears a noise,
Waah waah, waah waah.
(*Cup hand around ear.*)

Opens up the basket,
Baby inside!
Oh-oh! Oh-oh!
(*Clap hand onto mouth to show surprise.*)

Miriam is watching,
Asks princess…
Hmm-hmm, hmm-hmm…
(*Pretend to clear your throat and tap someone on shoulder.*)

Who'll look after Moses?
Gets her mum!
Yes yes! Yes yes!
(*Nod your head.*)

Mum looks after Moses.
God's good plan!
Hip-hip, hooray!
(*Everyone cheers!*)

 Jen Fawcett

 Exodus 2:1–10

 Follow this action rhyme with a prayer, with everyone saying 'Thank you, God!'

God, you keep us safe all the time. *Thank you, God.*
You looked after baby Moses and protected him. *Thank you, God.*
You promise to always look after us as well. *Thank you, God.*
You love each and every one of us! *Thank you, God.*

God's man, Moses

Back in Egypt God's people were sad
But God had a plan.
(*Spread hands as if opening a book.*)
They needed someone to get them out –
And God knew just the man!
(*Thumbs up.*)

Moses was looking after the sheep
But God had a different plan.
Moses thought he'd stay a shepherd –
But God knew he was the man!

Suddenly a bush caught fire,
(All part of God's plan),
Moses heard the voice of God –
God said, 'You're the man!'

Moses said, 'I can't do that!'
God said, 'Yes, you can!
You can – because I'll help you.'
And Moses said… 'I'm your man!'

 Alison Hulse

 Exodus 3:1 – 4:20

 Repeat the same actions in each verse.

Moses

Over the Red Sea

You are our God, you are our God,
Father God, Father God,
We'll sing to you for ever, we'll sing to you for ever,
You love us, you love us.

We were frightened, we were frightened,
Help us, God! Help us, God!
Sing to you for ever, sing to you for ever,
You saved us, you saved us.

You blew the sea back, you blew the sea back,
Made a path, made a path,
Sing to you for ever, sing to you for ever,
You saved us, you saved us.

You are mighty, you are mighty,
Big and strong, big and strong,
Sing to you for ever, sing to you for ever,
You save us, you save us.

You are our God, you are our God,
Always near, always near,
Sing to you for ever, sing to you for ever,
You are great, you are great.

 Sarah Jobson

 Exodus 15:1–21

 'Frère Jacques'

 Sing with plenty of enthusiasm and volume!

God's good rules

Ten good rules,
Ten good rules.
God gives to us,
(Point upward and then at one another.)
God gives to us.
He wants us all to live his way,
(Walk on the spot.)
To worship him, to sing and pray,
(Raise arms.)
And love each other every day.
(Cross arms over chest.)
Ten good rules.

 Christine Wright

 Exodus 19:16 – 20:17

 'Three blind mice'

Love God

This is what God says is right –
(Clap rhythmically.)
Love our God with all our might.
(Stretch arms upward; bring them down strongly.)
This is how we all should be –
(Clap again.)
Kind to friends and family.
(Hands with palm upwards held together; then sweep around to either side.)
This is what God says is right –
(Clap again.)
Love our God with all our might.
(Stretch arms upward; bring them down strongly.)

 Christine Wright

 Exodus 19:16 – 20:17

 'Twinkle, twinkle little star'

Joshua

Over the River Jordan

We're going to a new land!
We're not scared!
God is with us.
He knows the plan!
Joshua's leading us.
We're all following on behind.

Uh oh!
There's the River Jordan.
It's big, wide and deep.
We can't go over it.
We can't go under it.
We've got to go through it!

Splish, splash, splish, splash!
God's special box first.
We're all following on behind…
Look at the river!
The water's disappearing,
With every step we take.

Hooray, hooray, hooray!
God has helped us!
We're across the river!
God has helped us!
Joshua's leading us.
We're on the other side!

 Susie Matheson

 Joshua 3

 An adaptation of the traditional 'We're going on a bear hunt' game.

The Lord, strong and mighty

Our Lord God is God of all gods,
He is the Lord, strong and mighty.
He made the world, the sun, moon and stars.
He is the Lord, strong and mighty.
He made the mountains, he made the seas,
He is the Lord, strong and mighty.
He helped his people cross the River Jordan,
He is the Lord, strong and mighty.
We think he's great and want to praise him,
He is the Lord, strong and mighty.

 Susie Matheson

 Joshua 3

 A praise shout.

Marching!

Marching, marching, all around the wall,
Marching, marching, hear the trumpet call.
Shouting, shouting, on the seventh day,
Crash, the wall has fallen,
All shout: 'Hooray!'

 Tanya Ferdinandusz

 Joshua 6:1–20

 Join in with marching, shouting, crashing noises and cheering.

Gideon

God's plan for Gideon

Toot, toot, toot, let's all praise God!
Toot, toot, toot, let's all praise God!

God told Gideon what to do –
No big army – just a few.
Toot, toot, toot, let's all praise God!
Toot, toot, toot, let's all praise God!

Toot, toot, toot, the plan was made,
Gideon heard and then obeyed.
Toot, toot, toot, let's all praise God!
Toot, toot, toot, let's all praise God!

Toot, toot, toot, and shine the lights!
God helped Gideon win that night!
Toot, toot, toot, let's all praise God!
Toot, toot, toot, let's all praise God!

Bubbles for Leaders January–March 2006

Judges 7:1–22

Use your voices or play toy trumpets to make the tooting sounds.

Gideon

Thank you, Lord, for choosing Gideon,
Thank you, Lord, for choosing Gideon,
Thank you, Lord, for choosing Gideon,
Just as he was.

Thank you, Lord, for choosing me,
Thank you, Lord, for choosing me,
Thank you, Lord, for choosing me,
Just as I am.

Thank you, Lord, for choosing us,
Thank you, Lord, for choosing us,
Thank you, Lord, for choosing us,
Just as we are.

Alison Hulse

Judges 6:11–16,33–40

God's choice

(All walk around in a circle.)
God wants someone to help,
God wants someone to help,
Who will God choose?
God wants someone to help.

(Adult helper goes into the circle and acts being strong.)
A tall man, big and strong?
A tall man, big and strong?
No, that's not God's choice,
A tall man, big and strong.
(Adult rejoins circle.)

(Another helper goes into the circle and stands looking nervous.)
A young man, small and weak?
A young man, small and weak?
Yes, that is God's choice,
A young man, small and weak.
(Helper smiles.)

(Pause before final verse.)
God wants someone to help,
God wants someone to help,
God chooses me and you –
So do you want to help?

Bubbles for Leaders January–March 2006

Judges 6:11–16,33–40

'The farmer's in his den'

God's choice of Gideon appeared to be a strange one but God does not always do what we expect! Say how exciting it was for Gideon to be able to help God. Ask the children to think of ways they can help God. Perhaps by being kind and helpful? Perhaps by sharing and taking turns? God wants us to help him – wow! Start the game again and all walk around as you sing the final verse.

Samuel

Hannah's prayer

Hannah wanted a baby,
Hannah wanted a baby,
Hannah wanted a baby,
And what do you think she did?
She asked God for a baby,
She asked God for a baby,
She asked God for a baby,
A baby boy from God.

Hannah asked for a baby,
Hannah asked for a baby,
Hannah asked for a baby,
And what do you think God did?
He gave Hannah a baby,
He gave Hannah a baby,
He gave Hannah a baby,
A baby boy from God.

God gave Hannah a baby,
God gave Hannah a baby,
God gave Hannah a baby,
And what do you think she did?
She thanked God for the baby,
She thanked God for the baby,
She thanked God for the baby,
The baby boy from God.

The baby's name was Samuel,
The baby's name was Samuel,
The baby's name was Samuel,
And what do you think he did?
He grew up loving God,
He grew up loving God,
He grew up loving God,
The baby boy from God.

SALT 3 to 4+ April–June 2004

1 Samuel 1

'The bear went over the mountain'

Samuel's life for God

A life for God!
A life for God!
Samuel lived a life for God.

A little tiny baby, given by God,
And as he grew, his mother knew
He would live his life for God.
A life for God!
A life for God!
Samuel lived a life for God.

A child in the temple, listening to God,
A message heard, he told God's word,
He learned to serve his God.
A life for God!
A life for God!
Samuel lived a life for God.

A leader for the people, showing them God,
He helped them be a family
Who liked to worship God.
A life for God!
A life for God!
Samuel lived a life for God.

A brave and selfless leader, he always talked to God,
He chose a king, an important thing,
To do for them and God.
A life for God!
A life for God!
Samuel lived a life for God.

My life for God,
My life for God,
I want to live my life for God.

SALT 3 to 4+ April–June 2004

1 Samuel 1 – 10

The last verse of this rhyme gives everyone an opportunity to react and respond to Samuel's example.

David

God was with David

God was with David all day long,
With him to make him brave and strong.

God was there when he took his sheep,
Looking for grass on the mountains steep.

David knew God was taking care
Of each of us, all day, everywhere.

David wasn't afraid of the lion or the bear.
Why should he be, if God was there?

God was with him all the night,
When he slept out under the stars so bright.

Did you know God is taking care
Of each of us, all day, everywhere?

 Let's Join in! Scripture Union 1990 op

 1 Samuel 17:34–37; Psalm 23

Sons of Jesse

This is Samuel, this is Jesse,
(Wiggle thumbs to each other.)
This is Samuel, this is Jesse,
This is Samuel, this is Jesse,
Who will be the king?

One, two, three big sons of Jesse,
(Wiggle three fingers.)
One, two, three big sons of Jesse,
One, two, three big sons of Jesse,
Who will be the king?

One little, one little son of Jesse,
(Wiggle little finger.)
One little, one little son of Jesse,
One little, one little son of Jesse,
David will be king!

 Sheila Clift

 1 Samuel 16

 'Bobby Shaftoe'

 A finger rhyme.

David

King David danced

King David danced,
King David sang,
He danced and sang along the way.
King David praised
And thanked the Lord,
Just as we will do today!

 Let's Join in! Scripture Union 1990 op

 2 Samuel 6:12–15,21,22

 Use after telling the story of David bringing the Covenant Box back to Jerusalem. It links David's worship with our own. Adapt the last line to '…as we have done…' if saying the rhyme at the end of your session.

God said…

One thing God said, many years ago.
'David there will always be a king upon your throne.'
One thing God said,
Many, many, many, many, many years ago.

Two things God said, many years ago.
'David there will always be a king upon your throne.'
'He'll be a king who's good and fair.'
Two things God said,
Many, many, many, many, many years ago.

Three things God said, many years ago.
'David there will always be a king upon your throne.'
'He'll be a king who's good and fair.'
'He'll be born in Bethlehem.'
Three things God said,
Many, many, many, many, many years ago.

Four things God said, many years ago.
'David there will always be a king upon your throne.'
'He'll be a king who's good and fair.'
'He'll be born in Bethlehem.'
'Jesus is the promised king: all these things are true.'
Four things God said,
Many, many, many, many, many years ago.

 Geraldine Witcher

 2 Samuel 7; Isaiah 11:1–10; Micah 5:2–5; Matthew 1:1–17; Luke 3:23–38

 This rhyme explains the prophesied connection between David and Jesus for children who are not yet aware of time and chronology.

Solomon

Build a temple!

Build a temple, big and strong, e-i-e-i-o,
That's what David planned to do, e-i-e-i-o,
With wood and stone here,
Wood and stone there,
Here some wood, there some stone.
Everywhere some wood and stone,
Build a temple, big and strong, e-i-e-i-o.

Build a temple, big and strong, e-i-e-i-o,
Make it beautiful for God, e-i-e-i-o,
With lots of gold here,
And lots of jewels there,
Here some gold, there some jewels,
Everywhere gold and jewels,
Build a temple, big and strong, e-i-e-i-o.

Build a temple, big and strong, e-i-e-i-o,
The people came with gifts as well, e-i-e-i-o,
With lots of gifts here,
And lots of gifts there,
Here some gifts, there some gifts,
Everywhere gifts and gifts and gifts,
Build a temple, big and strong, e-i-e-i-o.

Build a temple, big and strong, e-i-e-i-o,
Sing a song of praise to God, e-i-e-i-o,
With praises here and praises there,
Here praises, there praises,
Everywhere sing God's praises,
Build a temple, big and strong, e-i-e-i-o.

Build a temple, big and strong, e-i-e-i-o,
The people praised God with their cheers, e-i-e-i-o,
With cheering here and cheering there,
Here a cheer, there a cheer,
Everywhere cheers and cheers and cheers,
Build a temple, big and strong, e-i-e-i-o.

 Kathryn Bishop

 1 Chronicles 29:1–20; 2 Chronicles 2 – 7; 1 Kings 5 – 9

 'Old Macdonald'

Elijah

Flap your wings!

Flap, flap, flap your wings,
Take Elijah meat.
Flappety, flappety, flappety, flappety,
God wants him to eat.

Flap, flap, flap your wings,
Take Elijah bread.
Flappety, flappety, flappety, flappety,
Yes, he must be fed.

Thank, thank, thank our God,
Let's all sing along.
Praise him, praise him, praise him, praise him
With our happy song.

 Ruth Dell

 1 Kings 17:2–6

 'Row, row, row your boat'

 Children will enjoy being ravens and feeding Elijah in the first two verses of this song.

Elijah and Ahab

King Ahab told his people,
'Build a bonfire, build a bonfire.
Ask Baal, ask Baal,
To light the fire, light the fire.'

Nothing happened, nothing happened,
Angry Ahab, angry Ahab!
No fire! No fire!
Baal couldn't light the fire.

Brave Elijah told the people.
'I'll build a bonfire, build a bonfire.
Ask God, ask God
To light the fire, light the fire.'

'Build a bonfire, build a bonfire,
Pour on water, pour on water.
Fire, fire! Fire, fire!
God is powerful! God is powerful!'

 Sheila Clift

 1 Kings 18:16–39

 'London's burning'

A quiet voice

God sent a strong wind
But God was stronger than that.
God is so strong.

God sent an earthquake
But God was stronger than that.
God is so strong.

God sent a blazing fire
But God was stronger than that.
God is so strong.

God spoke in a quiet voice
So Elijah would know
God was stronger than that.
God is so strong.

Strong enough for me,
Strong enough for you,
God is so strong.

 SALT 3 to 4+ July–September 2003

 1 Kings 19:1–18

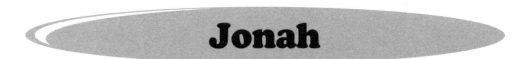

Jonah

Jonah

A man called Jonah has a job to do for God,
A job to do for God, a job to do for God;
A man called Jonah has a job to do for God,
But he doesn't want to do it!

He goes down to Joppa and he gets on board a ship,
Gets on board a ship, gets on board a ship,
He goes down to Joppa and he gets on board a ship,
That will take him far from Nineveh.

The big ship sails on the alley, alley-o,
The alley, alley-o; the alley, alley-o,
The big ship sails on the alley, alley-o,
With Jonah still on board it.

A big storm comes on the alley, alley-o,
The alley, alley-o; the alley, alley-o,
A big storm comes on the alley, alley-o,
And Jonah knows it's his fault.

The captain says, 'It'll never, never do,
Never, never do; never, never do.'
The captain says, 'It'll never, never do.'
And Jonah says, 'It's my fault!'

They throw Jonah into the deep blue sea,
Deep blue sea, deep blue sea.
They throw Jonah into the deep blue sea,
And everything is calm again.

A big fish swims by and swallows Jonah up,
Swallows Jonah up, swallows Jonah up.
A big fish swims by and swallows Jonah up,
And Jonah says, 'I'm sorry, God!'

The fish swims to land and spits Jonah out,
Spits Jonah out, spits Jonah out,
The fish swims to land and spits Jonah out,
And Jonah goes to Nineveh.

He tells the people there that they need to turn to
God,
Need to turn to God, need to turn to God,
He tells the people there that they need to turn to
God,
And to his surprise, they listen.

O thank you, Father God, you love and care for every-
one,
Care for everyone, care for everyone,
O thank you, Father God, you love and care for every-
one,
You've made each person special.

So help us, Father God, to know what we can do for
you,
We can do for you, we can do for you,
So help us, Father God, to know what we can do for
you,
As we share our world together.

 Jean Elliott

 Jonah 1 – 3

 'The big ship sails on the alley, alley-o'

 Choose three children to be Jonah, the captain and the fish.
Everyone else forms a circle with Jonah standing at the centre. The
captain and fish join and mime, as the song progresses.

Kings

King Jehoshaphat

An army came to fight the king,
Fight the king, fight the king,
An army came to fight the king,
A long time ago.

The king was scared and prayed to God,
Prayed to God, prayed to God,
The king was scared and prayed to God,
A long time ago.

God said to him, 'Just trust in me,
Trust in me, trust in me.'
God said to him, 'Just trust in me,'
A long time ago.

The people prayed and sang to God,
Sang to God, sang to God,
The people prayed and sang to God,
A long time ago.

The other army heard the sound,
Heard the sound, heard the sound,
The other army heard the sound,
A long time ago.

They were so scared, they ran away,
Ran away, ran away,
They were so scared, they ran away,
A long time ago.

The king thanked God, he danced and sang,
Danced and sang, danced and sang,
The king thanked God, he danced and sang,
A long time ago.

 Kathryn Bishop

 2 Chronicles 20:1–30

 'Here we go round the mulberry bush'

 Children will enjoy the apparent silliness of a story where singing and praising God is able to defeat a strong army!

Little baby Joash

Little baby Joash,
Hiding from the queen,
Hush, hush, hide away,
You must not be seen.

The baby's auntie took him,
Hid him well away.
Hush, hush, hide away,
You'll be king one day.

Standing in the Temple,
Joash, crowned as king.
Father God still cares for you,
Hear the people sing!

Little baby Joash,
God took care of you.
And, if we will trust him,
He'll care for us too.

 Let's Join in! Scripture Union 1990 op

 2 Kings 11:1–3; 2 Chronicles 22:10–12; 24:1

Josiah

God's word for Josiah

King Josiah was so sad.
People had been very bad,
Turned away from where God led,
They did not do what God said.
God's word is for me,
God's word is for me,
God's word is for me,
I know it is for me.

King Josiah was so good,
Obeying God all he could,
Tried to think what God would say,
Leading everyone God's way.
God's word is for me,
God's word is for me,
God's word is for me,
I know it is for me.

People cleaned up all the mess,
Making God's house look its best.
When they found God's holy book,
They just had to have a look.
God's word is for me,
God's word is for me,
God's word is for me,
I know it is for me.

God's instructions were not kept.
When he saw this, the king wept!
Straight away, Josiah saw
He must follow God's great law.
God's word is for me,
God's word is for me,
God's word is for me,
I know it is for me.

Now at last Josiah knew
What God wanted him to do.
He thanked God every day,
He knew how to live God's way.
God's word is for me,
God's word is for me,
God's word is for me,
I know it is for me.

Josiah saw he must obey,
So he said to God that day,
'I promise with all my heart,
From your words I'll not depart.'
God's word is for me,
God's word is for me,
God's word is for me,
I know it is for me.

God's words were, 'I am so good,
I'll help you do all you should.
Read my words and you will see
How I want you to praise me.
God's word is for me,
God's word is for me,
God's word is for me,
I know it is for me.

So, Josiah made a start,
Making sure he did his part,
Organising God's party,
Eating, sharing, happily.
God's word is for me,
God's word is for me,
God's word is for me,
I know it is for me.

God has given me a book,
In the Bible I can look.
Jesus calls me to obey,
I will follow him each day.
God's word is for me,
God's word is for me,
God's word is for me,
The Bible is for me!

 SALT 3 to 4+ October–December 2003

 2 Chronicles 34; 2 Kings 22 – 23

 'Jesus loves me, this I know'

Jeremiah

Jeremiah's poem

Jeremiah, who are you?
'Just a priest's son.'
Jeremiah, who are you?
'An unimportant one.'

God says, 'Jeremiah,
You're special though, to me.'
God says, 'Jeremiah,
I've chosen you, you see.'

Jeremiah, can you speak?
'I am much too young.'
Jeremiah can you speak?
'Tangled is my tongue.'

God says, 'Jeremiah,
I will help you today.'
God says, 'Jeremiah,
Here are my words to say.'

Jeremiah, can you see?
'A potter working clay.'
Jeremiah, can you see?
'He breaks, remakes today.'

God says, 'Jeremiah,
I'm the potter, you're the clay.'
God says, 'Jeremiah,
Tell people to obey.'

Jeremiah, can you read?
'I read the messages so.'
Jeremiah, can you read?
'The king won't listen, though.'

God says, 'Jeremiah,
Write the words once more.'
God says, 'Jeremiah,
Man can't destroy God's words.'

Jeremiah, where are you?
'Down the well so deep.'
Jeremiah, where are you?
'And the sides are steep!'

God says, 'Jeremiah,
You are in my care.'
God says, 'Jeremiah,
Help will soon be there.'

 Marjory Francis

 Jeremiah 1:1–10; 18:1–6; 36:1–32; 38:1–13

 Use the whole rhyme to tell Jeremiah's life story; or select verses to review separate incidents.

Jeremiah

Jeremiah, Jeremiah,
Spoke God's truth, spoke God's truth.
Said what God was saying, said what God was saying,
Loud and clear! Loud and clear!

We must listen, we must listen,
Hear God's truth, hear God's truth.
Hear what God is saying, hear what God is saying,
Loud and clear! Loud and clear!

 Dilys Gower

 Jeremiah 1:4–10

 'Frère Jacques'

 Jeremiah's role as a prophet was far from an easy one but he was faithful in speaking God's truth, even when he knew people would not listen. So, will we listen today?

Jeremiah

The king and the scroll

Once there was a bad king,
A bad king, a bad king.
(Crown on head, mean face.)
Once there was a bad king,
Who wouldn't listen to God.
(Use hands to cover ears.)

He said, 'I'll tear up God's Word,
God's Word, God's Word.'
He said, 'I'll tear up God's Word,
And throw it in the fire.'
(Tear first scroll.)

(Crown off, smiling face.)
God said, 'Baruch, write it down,
Write it down, write it down.'
(Mime writing.)
God said, 'Baruch, write it down.
God's Word will always stay.'
(Hold up second scroll and smile.)

 Christine Wright

 Jeremiah 36

 Wear a simple cardboard crown. Roll two lengths of paper to make scrolls, one to tear up and one to replace it.

Jeremiah in the well

Down, down, down, down,
Down to the bottom of the well.
Bump, bump, bump, bump,
Scraping down the side of the well.

Squelch, squelch, squelch, squelch,
In the mud at the bottom of the well.

Look up, up, up, up,
Faces round the top of the well.
Now down, down, down, down,
Comes a rope to the bottom of the well.

Squelch, squelch, squelch, squelch,
In the mud at the bottom of the well.

Pull, pull, pull, pull,
Slowly to the top of the well.
Up, up, up, up,
Jeremiah's at the top of the well.

 Geraldine Witcher

 Jeremiah 38:1–13

 Enjoy inventing actions and sound effects!

Daniel

Nebuchadnezzar and Daniel

None so proud and no one stronger,
Than King Nebuchadnezzar.
None so rich and no one grander,
Than King Nebuchadnezzar.

'Find me helpers, strong and clever,'
Said King Nebuchadnezzar.
'Teach them, feed them, make them fitter,'
Said King Nebuchadnezzar.

None so good and no one wiser
Than Daniel, God's messenger.
'This king's great, but God is greater,'
Said Daniel, God's messenger.

'I'll learn to be the king's helper,'
Said Daniel, God's messenger.
'But I can't eat the royal dinner,'
Said Daniel, God's messenger.

None so proud, but God is stronger
Than King Nebuchadnezzar.
None so rich, but God is greater
Than King Nebuchadnezzar.

 Christine Wright

 Daniel 1

 Children like strange new words and they will enjoy trying to say 'Nebuchadnezzar'.

Daniel

What will he do when he's tired and busy?
What will he do when he's tired and busy?
What will he do when he's tired and busy?
Daniel asks for God's help.
We know that God's the greatest,
We know that God's the greatest,
We know that God's the greatest,
And he always will be!

What will he do when the king says, 'Don't pray'?
What will he do when the king says, 'Don't pray'?
What will he do when the king says, 'Don't pray'?
Daniel asks for God's help.
We know that God's the greatest,
We know that God's the greatest,
We know that God's the greatest,
And he always will be!

What will he do when the lions are roaring?
What will he do when the lions are roaring?
What will he do when the lions are roaring?
Daniel asks for God's help.
We know that God's the greatest,
We know that God's the greatest,
We know that God's the greatest,
And he always will be!

 Christine Wright

 Daniel 6

 'What shall we do with the drunken sailor?'

 The repetitive style of this song means that children can join in easily.

Ezra and Nehemiah

Where we belong

'This is where we belong,' they said.
'We're the people of Jerusalem.
Our homes are here
And we don't *want* to *move*.
We don't *want* to *move*.
We don't *want* to *move* at all.'

'You have to come with us,' they said.
'We're the soldiers of Babylon.
Your homes are gone
And you've all *got* to *move*.
You've all *got* to *move*.
You've all *got* to *move* right now.'

'This is *not* where we belong,' they said.
'We belong in Jerusalem.
And just as God promised,
We just *want* to *go back*.
We *want* to *go back*.
We *want* to *go back* again.'

'*This* is where we belong,' they said.
'We're living again in Jerusalem.
Our homes are rebuilt
And we're glad we've come back.
God brought us back.
God brought us back. Praise him!'

 Christine Wright

 Ezra 1; 2:1,64–70

 This, and the next two rhymes, tells the story of the exile in a similar style, helping the children grasp the big, ongoing story of God's people.

Nowhere for God?

'Now that we're back in our homes,' they said,
'We've somewhere to live and somewhere to work
And somewhere to play,
But there's nowhere to praise
And nowhere to pray
And nowhere to talk about God.'

'Now that we're back in our homes,' they said,
'We need somewhere to meet and somewhere to learn
How we can please God.
But there's nowhere to praise
And nowhere to pray
And nowhere to talk about God.'

'Now that we're back in our homes,' they said,
'We want to think about God. His temple has gone,
But we'll build it again
And have somewhere to praise
And somewhere to pray
And somewhere to talk about God.'

'Now that the building's begun,' they said,
'We'll thank God for what he has done.'
So, singing and shouting, they said,
'There's somewhere to praise
And somewhere to pray
And somewhere to talk about God.
Praise God for what he has done!'

 Christine Wright

 Ezra 3

 This, the previous and next rhyme, tell the story of the exile in a similar style, helping the children grasp the big, ongoing story of God's people.

Ezra and Nehemiah

Building the Temple

'We want to build the Temple,' they said.
'We're the people of Jerusalem.
The work has begun,
But there's lots more to do.
There's lots more to do.
There's lots more to build and make.'

'We won't let you build the Temple,' they said.
'We're the enemies of Jerusalem.
The work has begun,
But we're going to stop you.
We're going to stop you.
We're going to stop you right now.'

'You can try to stop our building,' they said.
'We're the people of Jerusalem.
And God's on our side
And he won't let us down.
He won't let us down.
He won't let us down at all.'

'We've worked hard on the Temple,' they said.
'We're God's people in Jerusalem.
And we've done all our work.
And the Temple is finished.
The Temple is finished.
The Temple is finished. Praise God!'

 Christine Wright

 Ezra 4 – 6

 This, and the previous two rhymes, tells the story of the exile in a similar style, helping the children grasp the big, ongoing story of God's people.

Nehemiah, where are you?

Nehemiah, Nehemiah, where are you?
Here I am, here I am,
Waiting for news.

Nehemiah, Nehemiah, where are you?
Here I am, here I am,
Feeling so sad.

Nehemiah, Nehemiah, where are you?
Here I am, here I am,
Praying to God.

Nehemiah, Nehemiah, where are you?
Here I am, here I am,
Working for the king.

Nehemiah, Nehemiah, where are you?
Here I am, here I am,
Going to mend the walls.

 Christine Wright

 Nehemiah 1:1 – 2:10

Ezra and Nehemiah

Building and praising

We'll build the walls in the morning,
We'll build the walls in the morning,
We'll build the walls in the morning,
As God wants us to do.

We'll build the walls in the noon-time,
We'll build the walls in the noon-time,
We'll build the walls in the noon-time,
As God wants us to do.

We'll build the walls till the sun sets,
We'll build the walls till the sun sets,
We'll build the walls till the sun sets,
As God wants us to do.

We'll praise God in the morning,
We'll praise God in the morning,
We'll praise God in the morning,
We'll praise his holy name.

We'll praise God in the noon-time,
We'll praise God in the noon-time,
We'll praise God in the noon-time,
We'll praise his holy name.

We'll praise God in the evening,
We'll praise God in the evening,
We'll praise God in the evening,
We'll praise his holy name.

 Ruth Dell

 Nehemiah 2:11 – 3:32

 'Round and round the village'

 Improvise actions and join in with the repeating lines of the song.

Jerusalem's walls

Jerusalem's walls are tall and strong,
Tall and strong, tall and strong,
Jerusalem's walls are tall and strong,
God has helped us!

Now our homes are safe and sound,
Safe and sound, safe and sound,
Now our homes are safe and sound,
God has helped us!

Sing and dance and clap and shout,
Clap and shout, clap and shout,
Sing and dance and clap and shout,
God has helped us!

 Christine Orme

 Nehemiah 12:27–47

 'London Bridge is falling down'

Christmas

Mary and the angel

Mary was a quiet girl,
A quiet girl, a quiet girl,
Mary was a quiet girl.
Guess what happened next?

She saw a lovely angel,
An angel, an angel,
She saw a lovely angel!
Guess what happened next?

The angel said, 'God loves you,
God loves you, God loves you,'
The angel said, 'God loves you,
So don't be afraid!'

'You're going to have a baby,
A baby, a baby,
You're going to have a baby!'
Guess what happened next?

Mary said, 'A baby,
A baby, a baby?
How can I have a baby?'
Guess what happened next?

'Your baby comes from God,
From God, from God,
Your baby comes from God,
And Jesus is his name!'

Mary was so happy,
So happy, so happy,
Then Mary was so happy,
To know what God had done.

Mary was a quiet girl,
A quiet girl, a quiet girl,
Mary loved her baby,
And Jesus was his name.

 Bubbles for Leaders September–December 2004

 Luke 1:26–56

 Pause after each question to encourage a response from the children.

The angel came to see Mary

The angel came to see Mary,
She was most surprised.
'God is with you,
He's pleased with you,
So here I am to say:
A baby you'll have,
He will be God's Son,
Our King for evermore!'
The angel came to see Mary,
Praise God! Praise God! Praise God!

 Alison Dayer

 Luke 1:26–38

 'When Santa got stuck up the chimney'

Joseph's dream

Joseph had a dream one night,
When an angel, big and bright,
Told him, 'Joseph, it's all right –
You will marry Mary.
She will have a baby son,
He will be God's promised one.
He will love us, every one,
And his name is Jesus.'

 Margaret Spivey

 Matthew 1:18–25; Luke 2:1–7; Isaiah 7:14

 'Bobby Shaftoe'

Christmas

Rock the baby

Rock the baby in my arms.
(Mime rocking baby.)
Hold him snug and tight.
Lay him in his little bed
(Mime laying baby down.)
And gently kiss goodnight.
(Kiss hand.)

Dear Father God, keep all babies
(Mime rocking baby.)
In your loving care.
Thank you for sending Jesus
For us all to share.
(Mime holding baby out to others.)

 Christine Orme

 Luke 2:1–7; Matthew 1:18–25

 Ask the children to hold their arms in a way that looks as though they are cradling a baby. Suggest the children look at their cradled arms and think about baby Jesus.

This is the day

This is the day, this is the day, that the angel said, that the angel said,
'Mary's baby, Mary's baby,
Will be God's own Son, will be God's own Son.'
This is the day that the angel said,
'Mary's baby, will be God's own Son'.
This is the day, this is the day, that we sing about!

This is the day, this is the day, that God's Son is born, that God's Son is born.
Jesus is born, Jesus is born,
He is God's own Son, he is God's own Son.
This is the day that God's Son is born,
Jesus is born, he is God's own Son!
This is the day, this is the day, that we sing about!

 Angela Thompson

 Matthew 1:18–23; Luke 2:1–7

 'This is the day'

Sleep, baby Jesus

Sleep baby Jesus, cosy and warm,
Simeon holds you tight.
Anna has longed for you to be born,
Praying both day and night.

Come to thank God, come to thank God,
Jesus is God's own Son.
Come to thank God, come to thank God,
Jesus is God's own Son.

Sleep baby Jesus, cosy and warm,
While we give thanks for you.
Sleep baby Jesus, cosy and warm,
While we sing songs to you.

 Sheila Clift

 Luke 2:22–28

 'The Skye boat song' ('Speed, bonny boat')

 Sing the song through two or three times and let the children choose how to join in – they could sing, dance, rock a baby, sway, watch quietly.

Christmas

Here are the shepherds

Here are the shepherds, watching, waiting.
(Hold up fingers on right hand.)
Here is the angel, shining, showing.
(Hold up one finger on left hand.)
Here are the shepherds, trembling, shaking.
(Wiggle fingers on right hand.)
Here are the angels, singing, praising.
(Open and close fingers on left hand like a flash.)
Here are the shepherds, hurrying, scurrying.
(Move right hand quickly.)
Here is the baby, lying, sleeping.
(One horizontal finger on left hand.)
Here are the shepherds, rejoicing, praising.
(Open and close fingers on right hand like a flash.)
Here is Mary, pondering, wondering.
(Hold up one finger on left hand.)

 Priscilla Trood

 Luke 2:7–21

 A finger rhyme.

Shepherds' story

Dark, dark, dark, it's dark on the hillside.
Dark, dark, dark, alone with the sheep.
Dark, dark, dark, no stars and no sunshine.
Dark, dark, dark, I just want to sleep.

Light, light, light, a light in the night time.
Light, light, light, in the sky up above.
Light, light, light, a beautiful angel!
Light, light, light, he tells of God's love.

'News, news, news, good news,' says the angel.
'News, news, news, for everyone.
News, news, news, to make the people happy.
News, news, news, your Saviour has come.'

Praise, praise, praise, with angels on the hillside.
Praise, praise, praise, our God who loves us so.
Praise, praise, praise, for the birth of the baby.
Praise, praise, praise, as to Bethlehem we go.

Look, look, look, at the baby as he lies there.
Look, look, look, he is Christ the Lord.
Look, look, look, tell all that God has told us.
Look, look, look, he is worshipped and adored.

Run, run, run, through the streets back to the hillside.
Run, run, run, give the news to everyone.
Run, run, run, shout to God and sing his praises!
Run, run, run, this baby is God's Son!

 SALT 3 to 4+ October–December 2003

 Luke 2:8–20

 Pretend to be the shepherds on the night that Jesus was born.

Christmas

Simeon and Anna

Simeon went to the Temple,
Simeon went to the Temple,
Simeon went to the Temple,
And who do you think he saw?

He saw…
Mary, Joseph and Jesus,
Mary, Joseph and Jesus,
Mary, Joseph and Jesus.
Thank you, thank you God.

Anna went to the Temple,
Anna went to the Temple,
Anna went to the Temple,
And who do you think she saw?

She saw…
Mary, Joseph and Jesus,
Mary, Joseph and Jesus,
Mary, Joseph and Jesus.
Thank you, thank you God.

 Sheila Clift

 Luke 2:22–38

 'The bear went over the mountain'

 'Simeon' chooses three people to join him in the centre of a large circle. They hold hands and walk around while everyone else stands still and sings.

In the Temple

Simeon, Simeon, where have you been?
I've been to the Temple and guess what I've seen?

Simeon, Simeon, what did you see?
Mary and Joseph and their new baby.

Simeon, Simeon, what did you say?
I've waited and waited for this special day.

Simeon, Simeon, what did you do?
I sang and I prayed, 'Father God, I thank you.'

 Sheila Clift

 Luke 2:22–28

 'Pussy cat, pussy cat'

 Two leaders can sing or say these questions and answers.

Seeing Jesus

Simeon waiting, Simeon waiting,
To see God, to see God,
Jesus in the Temple, Jesus in the Temple,
Worship him, worship him.

Anna watching, Anna watching,
To see God, to see God,
Jesus with his mother, Jesus with his mother,
Worship him, worship him.

Wise men travelling, wise men travelling,
To see God, to see God,
See the little Jesus, see the little Jesus,
Worship him, worship him.

 Alison Irving

 Luke 2:22–28; Matthew 2:1–12

Christmas

The wise men

We're going on a journey,
Riding on our camels,
Back to where we came from,
When we saw the star.

We've seen the baby Jesus,
We've given him our presents,
Gold and myrrh and frankincense,
Now we're going home.

We won't go back to Herod,
The angel told us not to,
He wants to hurt the baby –
We'll go a different way!

We're going on a journey,
Riding on our camels,
Back to where we came from,
When we saw the star.

 Christine Orme

 Matthew 2:12–23

Jesus' family

We're going on a journey,
All the way to Egypt,
We have to get away now,
The angel said, 'Be quick!'

We're going to be going,
All the way to Egypt,
We have to get away now,
'Cos Herod's really cross!

We're taking all we have now,
All the way to Egypt,
We have to get away now,
While everyone's asleep.

God's promised to be with us,
All the way to Egypt.
We know we'll come back one day,
When God tells us it's safe.

 Christine Orme

 Matthew 2:13–23

Happy birthday, Jesus

What's the name of the baby? *Jesus, Jesus.*
He's a special baby. *He is God's Son.*

Who's the special baby? *Jesus, Jesus.*
He's a special baby. *He is God's Son.*

Happy birthday, Jesus. *Jesus, Jesus.*
Happy birthday, Jesus. *You are God's Son.*

Let's all sing for Jesus. *Jesus, Jesus.*
Happy birthday, Jesus. *You are God's Son.*

 SALT 3 to 4+ October–December 2002

 Luke 2:1–7; Matthew 1:18–25

 Children will learn the repeated answers quickly.

Jesus, the Son of God

Who is Jesus?

Is Jesus the Son of God? *Yes he is!*
Is Jesus the Saviour who dies on the cross? *Yes he is!*
Is Jesus the Lord who came back to life again? *Yes he is!*
Is Jesus the King who reigns in heaven? *Yes he is!*
Is Jesus the best friend ever? *Yes he is!*
Is he alive today? *Yes he is!*

 SALT 3 to 4+ April–June 2002

 Acts 2:22–47

Who is this man?

Who is this man?
Even the winds and waves obey him.
Who is this man?
He knows all our fears.
Who is this man?
He is with us in the storm.
Who is this man?
The Son of God!
The Lord of all!
Jesus!

Who is this man?
He knows when we are hungry.
Who is this man?
He knows when we are full.
Who is this man?
He gives us the food we need.
Who is this man?
The Son of God!
The Lord of all!
Jesus!

Who is this man?
He knows when we're ill.
Who is this man?
He knows when we're lonely.
Who is this man?
He makes sick people well.
Who is this man?
The Son of God!
The Lord of all!
Jesus!

Who is this man?
He spoke to the soldier.
Who is this man?
He did what was asked.
Who is this man?
He healed the man's servant.
Who is this man?
He helps us today.
Who is this man?
The Son of God!
The Lord of all!
Jesus!

 Adapted from *Let's Join in!*, Scripture Union 1990 op

 Matthew 8:1–13; Mark 1:40–45; Luke 5:12–16; Matthew 8:23–27; Luke 7:1–10; John 4:43–54; Matthew 15:32–39; Mark 8:1–10

 Select individual verses to retell parts of the story of Jesus; or use the whole rhyme to emphasise how 'Jesus' is the answer! Say the rhyme with two groups or two voices in a question-and-answer style. All say, 'Jesus!'

Jesus, the Son of God

The Son of God

Jesus always answers prayers,
Jesus always answers prayers,
Jesus always answers prayers,
He's the Son of God.
Jesus died then came alive,
Jesus died then came alive,
Jesus died then came alive,
He's the Son of God.

We can all be friends of Jesus,
We can all be friends of Jesus,
We can all be friends of Jesus,
He's the Son of God.
Jesus died then came alive,
Jesus died then came alive,
Jesus died then came alive,
He's the Son of God.

He has promised to be with us,
He has promised to be with us,
He has promised to be with us,
He's the Son of God.
Jesus died then came alive,
Jesus died then came alive,
Jesus died then came alive,
He's the Son of God.

He will help us to be like him,
He will help us to be like him,
He will help us to be like him,
He's the Son of God.
Jesus died then came alive,
Jesus died then came alive,
Jesus died then came alive,
He's the Son of God.

 Bubbles for Leaders January–March 2005

 Luke 24:1–12; Matthew 28:1–10; Mark 16:1–8; John 20:1–10

 'Bobby Shaftoe'

Jesus is!

Jesus is, Jesus is, Jesus is
WONDERFUL!
(Clap three times.)
Jesus is, Jesus is, Jesus is
OUR FRIEND!
(Raise hands.)

He loves us, he helps us
To know what's right and wrong.
He's kind, he cares.
He's with us all day long.

Jesus is, Jesus is, Jesus is
WONDERFUL!
(Clap three times.)
Jesus is, Jesus is, Jesus is
OUR FRIEND!
(Raise hands.)

 Let's Join in! Scripture Union 1990 op

 Matthew, Mark, Luke and John's Gospels

 The first verse can stand alone as a praise shout or prayer.

Jesus and his friends

Friends of Jesus

James, John, Peter and Andrew,
Will you be my special friends?
There's lots and lots of work to do,
I need all of you to help.

Thomas and Bartholomew,
Will you be my special friends?
There's lots and lots of work to do,
I need all of you to help.

Thaddaeus and Matthew,
Will you be my special friends?
There's lots and lots of work to do,
I need all of you to help.

Simon and James (number 2),
Will you be my special friends?
There's lots and lots of work to do,
I need all of you to help.

Philip, Judas, please come too,
Will you be my special friends?
There's lots and lots of work to do,
I need all of you to help.

 Kathleen Crawford

 Mark 3:13–19; Matthew 10:1–4; Luke 6:12–16

Matthew

Matthew, Matthew, sitting in the town,
Taking people's money, making people frown.
(Pretend to take money.)
Jesus, Jesus, helping everyone,
Went to Matthew's table, said to him, 'Come on.'
(Beckon.)
Matthew, Matthew, got up straight away,
Went to work with Jesus, helped him every day.
(Stand, smile and clap hands for joy.)

 SALT 3 to 4+ July–September 2002

 Matthew 9:9–13; Mark 2:13–17; Luke 5:27–32

The helpers went out two by two

The helpers went out two by two,
Two by two, two by two.
The helpers went out two by two.
They did what Jesus said.

They didn't carry lots of things,
(Stand still with hands held out, empty.)
Lots of things, lots of things.
They didn't carry lots of things.
They did what Jesus said.

They taught the people about God,
(Pretend to talk to people.)
About God, about God.
They taught the people about God.
They did what Jesus said.

 SALT 3 to 4+ July–September 2001

 Luke 9:1–6,10; Matthew 10:5–15; Mark 6:7–13

 'There was a princess long ago'

Jesus heals

See the woman

See the woman, lying still,
(Hold one index finger horizontally.)
She is feeling very ill.

Here is Jesus, wise and strong,
(Bring your other index finger forward, vertically.)
Peter's glad he came along.

Jesus touched the woman's hand.
(Touch fingers together lightly.)
At once, she smiled, felt better and – got up!
(Raise 'woman' finger upright.)

'I'm so much better now!' she said.
'I don't need to stay in bed!'
(Wiggle finger.)

 Chrissy Gower

 Mark 1:29–34; Matthew 8:14–17; Luke 4:38–41

 A finger rhyme.

At Peter's house

When Jesus went to Peter's house,
Who did he find in Peter's house?
Grandma who was ill in bed!
'Please will you help her?' Peter said.

When Jesus went to Peter's house,
Who did he heal in Peter's house?
Grandma who jumped out of bed,
And made a meal for them all instead!

 Bubbles for Leaders October–December 2005

 Mark 1:29–34; Matthew 8:14–17; Luke 4:38–41

Through the roof

One poor man was very ill,
Lying on his mat so still.
(One finger flat on palm.)
Four kind friends took the mat,
(Four fingers upright by palm.)
To the house where Jesus sat.
(Move hands.)

Four kind friends climbed to the roof,
(Move hands up.)
'We will see Jesus, and that's the truth!'
They made a hole and lowered the mat,
(Pretend to dig, then lower hand with finger on.)
Down to the place where Jesus sat.

Jesus looked at the man and said,
(One finger upright and one horizontal.)
'I will heal you – get off your bed!
All your sins are forgiven too,
So get up and walk! See what you can do!'

The man got up, no longer flat!
(Lift horizontal finger.)
How amazing to be off his mat!
His legs could walk! It felt so odd!
So home he danced, still praising God!
(Jiggle finger up and down.)

 Priscilla Trood

 Luke 5:17–26; Matthew 9:1–8; Mark 2:1–12

Jesus heals

The Roman officer

Oh, the Roman officer
Had soldiers brave and bold.
He said, 'Go here,' he said, 'Go there,'
They did as they were told.
And when he said, 'Come,' they came;
And when he said, 'Go,' they went;
He knew they followed his commands
And marched where they were sent.

Oh, the Roman officer
Had a servant sick in bed.
He'd heard of Jesus, knew his power,
'Please help my friend,' he said.
'For you have the power to save
And you have the power to heal.
You only have to say the word
And my servant will be well.'

Oh, the Roman officer,
His faith made Jesus glad.
'I love when people trust my power,
Of course I'll help the lad.'
For Jesus has power to save,
And Jesus has power to heal.
He stood far off and said the word
And the servant was quite well!

Oh, the Roman officer
Shows us how to behave.
He trusted Jesus, knew his power,
Knew Jesus' love can save.
For Jesus has power to help,
We only have to pray,
Please Jesus come and help us now,
We need your power today!

 Mary Houlgate

 Luke 7:1–10; Matthew 8:5–13; John 4:43–54

 'The grand old Duke of York'

 March and sing!

A man with leprosy

(Stand with heads bowed, hugging yourselves.)
This poor man was very ill, very ill, very ill,
This poor man was very ill, very ill.

(Make 'shoo-ing' movements.)
Everyone said, 'Go away, go away, go away.'
Everyone said, 'Go away, go away.'

(Kneel.)
He asked Jesus, 'Make me well, make me well, make me well.'
He asked Jesus, 'Make me well, make me well.'

(Stand and reach out one hand.)
Jesus touched him, made him well, made him well, made him well,
Jesus touched him, made him well, made him well.

 Christine Orme

 Matthew 8:1–4; Mark 1:40–45; Luke 5:12–16

 'London Bridge is falling down'

 Children's involvement in role play can become intense, so think carefully before asking children to act out the first two verses of this song: it is important that the children do not feel rejected themselves.

Jesus heals

A man by the road

A man sits at the roadside,
A man sits at the roadside,
A man sits at the roadside,
He's blind, he cannot see.

He shouts out loud to Jesus,
He shouts out loud to Jesus,
He shouts out loud to Jesus,
'Please Jesus! Make me see!'

Jesus stops and heals him,
Jesus stops and heals him,
Jesus stops and heals him,
And Jesus makes him see.

He skips along with Jesus,
He laughs and sings for Jesus,
He dances thanks to Jesus,
For Jesus made him see!

 Priscilla Trood

 Luke 18:35–43; Matthew 20:29–34; Mark 10:46–52

 'Round and round the village'

Meeting Jesus

When Jesus met the blind man, Jesus helped him see.
Thank you, Jesus, that we can see.
(Ask the children what they can see, and encourage each of them to say, 'Thank you, Jesus, that I can see...')

When Jesus met the deaf man, Jesus helped him hear.
Thank you, Jesus, that we can hear.
(Ask the children what they can hear and join in saying, 'Thank you, Jesus, that I can hear...')

When Jesus met the lame man, Jesus helped him walk and jump.
Thank you, Jesus, that we can walk and jump.
(Let all the children walk and jump.)

When Jesus met the girl, Jesus helped her live to run and play and shout.

Thank you, Jesus, that we can run and play and shout!
THANK YOU, JESUS!

 Ali Matchett

 Jesus' healing miracles, for example, Luke 18:35–43; Mark 7:31–37; Luke 5:17–26; Luke 8:40–56

 Be sensitive to any children who have disabilities, and if you have a wide range of physical development within the group.

Jesus is the best

A man asked Jesus to help him.
(All hold out one hand in front.)
Jesus touched him
(Hold out the other hand.)
And made him better.
(Cross arms over your chest.)
And now the man was well!
(Lift both hands high.)

Jesus you are good.
(All hold out one hand in front.)
Jesus you are great.
(Hold out the other hand.)
Jesus you love us.
(Cross arms over your chest.)
Jesus you're the best!
(Lift both hands high.)

 Christine Orme

 Matthew 8:1–4; Mark 1:40–45; Luke 5:12–16

 What do the children think the man might have said to Jesus? What would you say to him? Pray together now.

What Jesus did

A wedding at Cana

We're going to a wedding in Cana, Galilee.
Jesus came to ask his friends,
'Will you come with me?'
We're putting on our smartest clothes and combing out our hair,
There'll be singing, dancing, lots of fun and food and wine to share.

But oh dear!
The bridegroom shakes his head.
Jesus' mother gives a sigh.
'There's no wine left,' she says.
Jesus whispers, 'I can help.
I feel so sad for him.
Fill six jars with water
And fill them to the brim.'

The jars are overflowing:
The bridegroom has a taste.
He smiles, he nods, he looks so pleased –
He has a happy face.
The water in the jars has changed
Into delicious wine!
Jesus saves the wedding feast.
He's so special and so kind!

 Sheila Clift

 John 2:1–12

Jesus goes to a wedding

(All walk around the room to go to the wedding.)
Jesus went to a wedding today,
Jesus went to a wedding today,
Jesus went to a wedding today.
Let's all shout out, 'Hooray!'

(All shake heads and look sad.)
Mary saw the wine had gone,
Mary saw the wine had gone,
Mary saw the wine had gone,
Said, 'Jesus, help them please.'

(Pretend to fill up the jars.)
'Fill these water jars right up,
Fill these water jars right up,
Fill these water jars right up,'
Jesus told the men.

(Pretend to drink.)
He turned the water into wine,
He turned the water into wine,
He turned the water into wine,
The best they'd ever tried.

(Everyone dances around.)
Everyone is happy now,
Everyone is happy now,
Everyone is happy now,
Let's all shout out, 'Hooray!'

(Sing and shout.)
Sing to Jesus – shout, 'Hooray!'
Sing to Jesus – shout, 'Hooray!'
Sing to Jesus – shout, 'Hooray!'
Hooray, hooray, hooray!

 Ali Matchett

 John 2:1–12

 'Thank you, Lord, for this fine day'

 The verse pattern is easy to pick up but you will need to lead strongly, as the children are likely to be concentrating on what they are doing more than joining in with the words.

What Jesus did

Food to eat

The people came to see Jesus,
See Jesus, see Jesus.
The people came to see Jesus,
On that day.

Jesus talked about God's love,
About God's love, about God's love,
Jesus talked about God's love,
On that day.

The people wanted food to eat,
Food to eat, food to eat,
The people wanted food to eat,
On that day.

Five loaves, two fish was all they had,
All they had, all they had,
Five loaves, two fish was all they had,
On that day.

Jesus thanked God for the food,
For the food, for the food,
Jesus thanked God for the food,
On that day.

Everyone had lots to eat,
Lots to eat, lots to eat,
Everyone had lots to eat,
On that day.

Now we all say, 'Thank you, God',
'Thank you, God,' 'Thank you, God',
Now we all say, 'Thank you, God',
Here today.

 Ali Matchett

 John 6:1–15, 30; Matthew 14:13–21; Mark 6:30–44; Luke 9:10–17

 'The wheels on the bus'

Bread and fish

There were hundreds of people, thousands and thousands,
All listening to Jesus on the hill one day.
It was getting late and they all felt hungry,
But nobody wanted to go away.

All they had for those thousands and thousands,
Was fresh-made bread and a fish or two.
Jesus took the food and he prayed to his father,
And everyone wondered, 'What will Jesus do?'

He shared the food out with thousands and thousands,
The grown-ups and the children and the toddlers too.
Plenty for everyone – and more left over –
'Bread and fish for you and you and you and you.'

 Maggie Barfield

 Matthew 15:32–39; Mark 8:1–10

 'There are hundreds of sparrows'

What Jesus did

Jesus and the storm

The sails on the boat go up and down,
Up and down, up and down,
The sails on the boat go up and down,
All night long.

The oars on the boat go splish and splash,
Splish and splash, splish and splash,
The oars on the boat go splish and splash,
All night long.

The waves round the boat go crash, crash, crash,
Crash, crash, crash; crash, crash, crash,
The waves round the boat go crash, crash, crash,
All night long.

The people in the boat go wobble, wobble, wobble,
Wobble, wobble, wobble; wobble, wobble, wobble,
The people in the boat go wobble, wobble, wobble,
All night long.

Jesus in the boat goes *zzzz, zzzz, zzzz,*
Zzzz, zzzz, zzzz; zzzz, zzzz, zzzz,
Jesus in the boat goes *zzzz, zzzz, zzzz,*
All night long.

The people in the boat shout, 'Wake up please,
Wake up please, wake up please!'
The people in the boat shout, 'Wake up please!'
All night long.

Jesus in the boat says, 'Waves be still,
Waves be still, waves be still.'
Jesus in the boat says, 'Waves be still,'
All night long.

Jesus in the boat says, 'Wind be calm,
Wind be calm, wind be calm.'
Jesus in the boat says, 'Wind be calm,'
All night long.

The wind and the waves go calm and still,
Calm and still, calm and still,
The wind and the waves go calm and still,
All night long.

The people in the boat ask, 'Who is he?
Who is he, who is he?'
The people in the boat ask, 'Who is he?'
All night long.

 Tiddlywinks: The Big Purple Book, Scripture Union 2003

 Matthew 8:23–27; Mark 4:35–41; Luke 8:22–25

 'The wheels on the bus'

What Jesus did

Walking on the water

Jesus fed five thousand people,
Then he went to pray.
His friends all got into a boat
And then they rowed away.

The wind soon started howling
And the waves began to splash!
The friends of Jesus all felt scared
And hoped they wouldn't crash.

Jesus walked out to the boat
On top of the watery sea!
His friends could not believe their eyes!
What was it they could see?

'It's me!' called Jesus, through the storm,
Walking to the boat.
Peter wanted to go to him
So he took off his coat.

He jumped into the water
And *he* walked upon the sea!
Then Peter started sinking
And shouted, 'Lord, save me!'

Jesus reached out his hand to Peter
And pulled him from the sea.
'Why do you doubt?' asked Jesus,
'Just keep on trusting me!'

 SALT 3 to 4+ July–September 2003

 Matthew 14:22–33; Mark 6:45–52; John 6:15–21

Two pennies

The Temple offering boxes
Were standing in a row.
Along came a rich man
Who shouted out, 'Hello!
Look at how much gold I have,
How much I give away.
Can you see how good I am?
That's what I want to say!'

The Temple offering boxes
Were standing in a row.
Along came a widow
Who did not say, 'Hello!'
Her clothes were poor and worn.
She was hungry every day,
But she dropped two pennies
In the box and quietly walked away.

The Temple offering boxes
Were standing in a row.
Jesus watched the people
Walking to and fro.
'I tell you truly now...' he said,
And this is what he told,
'...God loves the woman's pennies
More than all the rich man's gold'.

 Sheila Clift

 Luke 21:1–4; Mark 12:41–44; Matthew 6:1–4

 'Sing a song of sixpence'

Meeting Jesus

Zacchaeus

Small Zacchaeus climbed a tree,
(Mime climbing.)
Oh what can he see?
('Scan' horizon.)
He sees people everywhere,
(Point with finger.)
As crowded as can be.
(Make self as thin as possible.)
With a hustle bustle here,
(Wriggle elbows and shoulders.)
And a hustle bustle there,
(Wriggle.)
Here a hustle,
(Wriggle.)
There a bustle,
(Wriggle.)
Everywhere a hustle bustle.
(Wriggle energetically.)
Small Zacchaeus climbed a tree,
('Climb'.)
Oh what can he see?
('Scan'.)

He sees Jesus on the ground,
(Point down.)
Underneath the tree.
'I want to come to your home,
Come and follow me!'
(Beckon.)
With a 'Praise God' here,
(Raise one arm.)
And a 'Hooray' there,
(Shout, raise other arm.)
Here a 'Praise God',
(Shout, raise first arm.)
There a 'Hooray!'
(Shout, raise second arm.)
Everywhere a 'Praise God, Hooray!'
(Shout, raise both arms.)
Zacchaeus climbed down from the tree,
('Climb'.)
'Jesus, he loves me!'
(Hug self.)

 Alison Irving

 Luke 19:1–10

 'Old MacDonald'

Enjoy using your bodies in story telling and worship.

Woman of Samaria

A woman from Samaria
Met Jesus at the well
And she was filled with wonder
At the things that he could tell.

He told her all about her life,
Her family and friends.
He told her of our Father God
And of the love he sends.

The woman from Samaria
Left Jesus at the well.
She went into the marketplace
To find her friends to tell.

The people came to meet him
And listened to his word.
They loved him and they called him
'The Saviour of the world'.

 Sheila Clift

 John 4:3–42

 Hold hand or finger puppets to show what happened when Jesus met the woman.

Meeting Jesus

Come with me

There once was a rich and very kind man,
Very kind man, very kind man,
There once was a rich and very kind man,
Long ago.

Jesus said, 'Leave your things behind,
Things behind, things behind.'
Jesus said, 'Leave your things behind,
And come with me.'

The rich man said, 'I can't do that,
Can't do that, can't do that.'
The rich man said, 'I can't do that,
To come with you.'

Jesus says, 'Please come with me,
Come with me, come with me.'
Jesus says, 'Please come with me,
Be my friend.'

Will you be a friend of God,
Friend of God, friend of God?
Will you be a friend of God,
Friend of God?

 Angela Thompson

 Mark 10:17–31; Matthew 19:16–30; Luke 18:18–30

 'There was a princess long ago'

 The final verse makes an offer to us. The rich man said, 'No'. What will we say?

Tell us, Simon Peter

Tell us what you've SEEN, Simon Peter.
Tell us what you've SEEN.
'I've seen Jesus care for children,
Healing people, feeding crowds.
Everything has been amazing.
That is what I've seen.'

Tell us what you've HEARD, Simon Peter.
Tell us what you've HEARD.
'I've heard Jesus telling stories,
Teaching people, calming storms.
Everything has been amazing.
That is what I've heard.'

Tell us what you've DONE, Simon Peter.
Tell us what you've DONE.
'I have been a friend of Jesus,
Walking with him, listening hard.
Everything has been amazing.
That is what I've done.'

Tell us what you've LEARNED, Simon Peter.
Tell us what you've LEARNED.
'I believe that God sent Jesus.
He's the one we're waiting for.
I know Jesus is amazing.
That is what I've learned.'

 Christine Wright

 Matthew 16:13–28; Mark 8:27–30; Luke 9:18–21

 How did Peter know who Jesus was? This rhyme reviews some of the evidence.

Meeting Jesus

Martha and Mary

Here is busy Martha,
(Hold up one thumb.)
Working all the day.
(Wiggle thumb around.)
Too busy to listen to Jesus,
Too busy to hear what he says.

Here is listening Mary,
(Hold up other thumb.)
Listening all the day.
(Keep thumb still.)
Wanting to listen to Jesus,
Wanting to hear what he says.

Will I be too busy
To hear what Jesus says?
Or will I listen to him?
Which will I do today?

 Adapted from *Let's Join in!* Scripture Union 1990 op

 Luke 10:38–42

 A finger rhyme.

Our friend

Jesus wants us all to know
We can be his friends,
Just like Mary we can know,
Jesus is our friend.

 Bubbles for Leaders April–June 2006

 Luke 10:38–42

 'Row, row, row your boat'

 Stand in a circle and sing the song together. Hold hands and skip round in one direction while the leaders 'la' the first two lines of the tune; skip back again for the remaining lines.

Stand still again and sing the song again.

Name each child as you say in turn, '*Richard*, Jesus wants you to know you can be his friend.' Do not press such young children for a direct response to this offer but be alert for individuals wanting to say what they think and feel about Jesus being a friend. Sing and skip again.

Glad to see Jesus

Lots of children went to see Jesus.
(Wave fingers.)
Some children walked to see Jesus.
(Walk two fingers along your other arm.)
Some children ran to see Jesus.
('Run' two fingers along arm.)
All the children clapped their hands
(Clap!)
Because they were so glad to see Jesus.
(Cheer!)

 Dilys Gower

 Matthew 19:13–15; Mark 10:13–16; Luke 18:15–17

Stories Jesus told

The farmer and his seeds

The farmer sowed his seeds,
The farmer sowed his seeds,
Up, down, all around,
The farmer sowed his seeds.

Some seeds fell on the path,
Some seeds fell on the path,
The birds flew down and ate them up,
Some seeds fell on the path.

Some seeds fell on the rocks,
Some seeds fell on the rocks,
The sun was much too hot for them,
Some seeds fell on the rocks.

Some seeds fell near the thorns,
Some seeds fell near the thorns,
The thorns were much too strong for them,
Some seeds fell near the thorns.

Some seeds fell in good soil,
Some seeds fell in good soil,
They grew up tall and strong and straight,
Some seeds fell in good soil.

 Sue Andrews

 Mark 4:1–9; Matthew 13:1–9; Luke 8:4–8

 'The farmer's in his den'

 Improvise actions: pretend to be the farmer or the seeds.

Rain and sun

When God sees soil is hard,
Or when it's dry and brown,
If the soil is very thirsty,
God makes the rain come down.

When the soil is very wet,
The little seeds will die.
God's sunshine dries the earth and so
The plants can grow up high.

I'm glad we've got the good, deep earth,
And lots of seeds to sow.
I'm glad we've got the rain and sun
And tasty plants to grow.

 SALT 3 to 4+ October–December 2002

 Mark 4:1–9; Matthew 13:1–9; Luke 8:4–8

Stories Jesus told

Growing seeds

God gives the rain and God gives the sun.
(Crouch down and…)
Hey-ho and up they go, God makes them grow.
(…make a 'star jump'.)

The seeds start to swell, the seeds start to swell,
(Cup hands together and then move hands apart slowly.)
Hey-ho and up they grow, the seeds start to swell.
God gives the rain and God gives the sun.
Hey-ho and up they go, God makes them grow.

The little roots grow down, the little roots grow down,
(Hold hands downwards and wiggle fingers.)
Hey-ho and down they go, the little roots grow down.
God gives the rain and God gives the sun.
Hey-ho and up they go, God makes them grow.

The little leaves sprout out, the little leaves sprout out,
(Stretch arms out slowly from sides of body, open out hands flat as leaves.)
Hey-ho and up they go, the little leaves sprout out.
God gives the rain and God gives the sun.
Hey-ho and up they go, God makes them grow.

 Sue Andrews

 Mark 4:26–29

 'The farmer's in his den'

 Stand in a large circle, with plenty of space to do the actions.

Two men praying

Two men went to pray,
Praying in the Temple,
One man, two men, praying there,
Praying in the Temple.

One man stood so bold,
Praying in the Temple.
'Look at me! I'm very good!'
Praying in the Temple.

One man stood alone,
Praying in the Temple.
'I'm sorry, God, for doing wrong.'
Praying in the Temple.

We can talk to God,
Talk to God together.
Let's all pray to God right now,
Talk to God together.

We can talk to God,
Talk to God together.
Loudly, loudly, talk to God,
Talk to God together.

 Bubbles for Leaders January–March 2005

 Luke 18:9–14

 'One man went to mow'

 Repeat the last verse, varying the words in italics, for example, softly, jumping, clapping, standing, sitting, with others, sadly. Follow up each repeat with a short prayer time.

Stories Jesus told

Come to the party

'Come to my party,' he said.
'Everything's ready for you.
My friends and I will have such fun.
Come to my party,' he said.

No friends are going to come.
They've got other things they must do.
No friends to come, there'll be no fun.
Nobody's able to come.

'Come to my party,' he said.
'Everything's ready and so,
If you are poor or hurt or sad,
Come to my party,' he said.

New friends have come to his house.
The party is ready to start.
There's food and drink and lots of fun.
New friends have come to the house.

 Christine Wright

 Luke 14:15–24; Matthew 22:1–10

 'Hickory dickory dock'

Ten small oil lamps

Ten small oil lamps burning in the night,
Ten small oil lamps make the house so bright.
And if ten small oil lamps are going to stay alight,
There'll be ten young bridesmaids with a shining light.

Five small oil lamps burning in the night,
Five small oil lamps make the house so bright,
Just five small oil lamps are going to stay alight,
Only five young bridesmaids have a shining light.

 Christine Wright

 Matthew 25:1–13

 'Ten green bottles'

 Hold up and wiggle ten or five fingers according to the number in each verse. Remind the children that only five of the bridesmaids had extra oil for their lamps. The other five were not ready when the bridegroom came.

Stories Jesus told

One hundred sheep

One hundred sheep I had with me,
(Spread arms wide, then point to self.)
But one has gone astray.
(Point into distance.)
Where, oh where, can that sheep be?
(Shrug shoulders.)
I must find her today.

Everywhere I seemed to look,
(Look around.)
By river, hill and tree.
Then I saw her by the brook –
('See' sheep.)
Happy, happy me!
(Smile and point to self.)

 Let's Join In! Scripture Union 1990 op

 Luke 15:3–6; Matthew 18:12–14

 Pretend to be the shepherd as you join in the actions with this rhyme.

One little sheep

One little sheep, he went to play.
One little sheep, he went away.
The good, kind shepherd, he searched all day.
When he found the sheep he shouted, 'Hooray!'

 Elizabeth Whitworth

 Luke 15:3–6; Matthew 18:12–14

 Move around the room, looking for your lost sheep; shout out when you find it.

The lost coin

'Wherever can it be?' said the woman,
When she lost a silver coin.
'I've only got nine, I should have ten.
(Count ten fingers, then nine.)
Wherever can it be?'

'Wherever can it be?' said the woman,
And she went to light her lamp.
She swept the floor, looked under the chairs.
'Wherever can it be?'

'Wherever can it be?' said the woman,
As she looked behind the door.
She searched the room, looked under the beds.
'Wherever can it be?'

'There it is!' said the woman happily,
When she found her silver coin.
(Make a circle with thumb and forefinger.)
She was so glad she jumped for joy – and she
Asked all her friends to tea!

 Let's Join In! Scripture Union 1990 op

 Luke 15:8–10

 Improvise actions as you mime helping the woman search for her coin.

Stories Jesus told

A loving father

There once was a hard-working father
Who worked on his farm with his sons.
But one son was fed up with working –
He wanted to have lots of fun.

He said, 'Dad, I want all my money.
I'm going to leave right away.'
His father was sad, for he loved him,
And wished that his young son would stay.
(Stride briskly to the town.)

The son went away to the city;
Had fine clothes and parties and friends.
(Mime having a party.)
But nobody wanted to know him,
When his money had come to an end.
(All turn their backs.)

He needed some help; he was hungry,
But nobody wanted to know.
He got a job down on a pig farm –
There seemed nowhere else he could go.
(All sit down and pretend to be sad.)

'I'm going to go home to my father,'
The young man decided at last.
'I'll tell him that I'm very sorry.
He might give me a job if I ask.'
(Walk slowly back home.)

Now, back home, his father was waiting,
(He'd been waiting and watching each day),
Longing and loving and hoping,
From the time that his son went away.

Then one day his long wait was over –
He saw a thin figure he knew!
He ran to his son and he hugged him!
(Leader runs towards group.)
The son hugged his father back, too!
(Everyone walks brightly back home.)

At the farm there was such a great party –
Such music and dancing around –
And the happiest man was the father,
For his son who was lost, had been found!
(Dance!)

 Maggie Barfield

 Luke 15:11–24

Stories Jesus told

The kind traveller

A man comes walking, walking along.
Walking along, walking along.
A man comes walking, walking along,
Walking along the road.

Nasty robbers, hurting the man,
Hurting the man, hurting the man.
Nasty robbers, hurting the man,
Leaving him by the road.

See the poor man, lying just there,
Lying just there, lying just there.
See the poor man, lying just there,
Lying beside the road.

An important man comes walking along,
Walking along, walking along.
An important man comes walking along,
Walking along the road.

Sees the poor man, lying just there,
Lying just there, lying just there.
Sees the poor man, lying just there,
Lying beside the road.

The important man keeps walking along,
Walking along, walking along.
The important man keeps walking along,
Walking along the road.

A clever man comes walking along,
Walking along, walking along.
A clever man comes walking along,
Walking along the road.

Sees the poor man, lying just there,
Lying just there, lying just there,
Sees the poor man, lying just there,
Lying beside the road.

The clever man keeps walking along,
Walking along, walking along.
The clever man keeps walking along,
Walking along the road.

A kindly man comes riding along,
Riding along, riding along.
A kindly man comes riding along,
Riding along the road.

Sees the poor man, lying just there,
Lying just there, lying just there.
Sees the poor man, lying just there,
Lying beside the road.

The kind man stops and helps the poor man,
Helps the poor man, helps the poor man.
The kind man stops and helps the poor man,
Helps him, beside the road.

 Bubbles for Leaders January–March 2006

 Luke 10:25–37

 'Big floppy teddy bears'

A gift for Jesus

Perfume for Jesus

Jesus loves me so what shall I do?
(Cross heart.)
What shall I do? What shall I do?
Jesus loves me so what shall I do,
To show I love him too?
(Cross heart.)

I will kneel down and kiss both his feet,
(Kneel.)
Kiss both his feet, kiss both his feet.
I will kneel down and kiss both his feet,
To show I love him too.
(Cross heart.)

Jesus forgives me so what shall I give?
(Cup hands.)
What shall I give? What shall I give?
Jesus forgives me so what shall I give,
To show I love him too?
(Cross heart.)

I will give him this precious perfume,
(Cup hands.)
Precious perfume, precious perfume.
I will give him this precious perfume,
To show I love him too.
(Cross heart.)

 Priscilla Trood

 Luke 7:36–50

 'Here we go round the mulberry bush'

A present for Jesus

A woman had a bottle, a very special bottle,
(Child/leader holds a real or pretend bottle carefully.)
And in that bottle was some perfume.
(Point to bottle, smile.)
The woman took the bottle, the very special bottle,
(Mime opening bottle.)
And poured the perfume over Jesus.
(Mime.)

Jesus' friends knew the bottle, the very special bottle,
Had cost the woman lots of money.
(Pretend to count coins.)
They could have sold the bottle, the very special bottle,
And given the money to the poor.
(Shake head, and look disapproving.)

But Jesus said the bottle, the very special bottle,
Was a present that made him happy.
(Smile.)
Yes, Jesus said the bottle, the very special bottle,
Was a present that made him happy.

 Kathleen Crawford

 Matthew 22:34–40; Mark 12:28–34; Luke 10:25–28; Matthew 26:6–13; Mark 14:3–9; John 12:1–8

Palm Sunday

Jesus on a donkey

We're clapping, we're cheering,
Jesus is appearing.
Hosannas ring, here comes our king,
A-riding on a donkey.

We're waving, we're prancing,
Children are all dancing.
Hosannas ring, here comes our king,
A-riding on a donkey.

 Sue Andrews

 Matthew 21:1–11; Mark 11:1–11; Luke 19:28–38; John 12:12–19

 'It's raining, it's pouring'

 Join the people in the crowd and welcome Jesus!

Jesus, our king

Jesus our king, we welcome you!
We welcome you!
Jesus our friend, we love you!
We love you!
Jesus our helper, we thank you!
We thank you!
Jesus our saviour, we praise you!
We praise you!

 Mary Houlgate

 Matthew 21:1–11; Mark 11:1–11; Luke 19:28–38; John 12:12–19

 Say this prayer quietly or shout it out.

Riding on a donkey

He'll be riding on a donkey, when he comes,
He'll be riding on a donkey, when he comes,
He'll be riding on a donkey, riding on a donkey,
Riding on a donkey, when he comes.

Our coats can be his saddle, when he comes,
Our coats can be his saddle, when he comes,
Our coats can be his saddle, coats can be his saddle,
Coats can be his saddle, when he comes,

We'll lay leaves and coats before him, when he comes,
We'll lay leaves and coats before him, when he comes,
We'll lay leaves and coats before him, leaves and coats before him,
Lay leaves and coats before him, when he comes.

We will shout, 'Hooray! Hosanna!' when he comes,
We will shout, 'Hooray! Hosanna!' when he comes,
We will shout, 'Hooray! Hosanna!' shout, 'Hooray! Hosanna!'
Shout, 'Hooray! Hosanna!' when he comes.

 Mary Houlgate

 Matthew 21:1–11; Mark 11:1–11; Luke 19:28–38; John 12:12–19

 'She'll be coming round the mountain'

Palm Sunday

He's off to Jerusalem!

Sing a song and shout for joy,
Happy is each girl and boy.
Shout for King Jesus!
He's off to Jerusalem!

He's off to Jerusalem!
He's off to Jerusalem!
Riding on a donkey,
He's off to Jerusalem!

It was early in the day,
Jesus started on his way.
Wave all your branches!
He's off to Jerusalem!

He's off to Jerusalem!
He's off to Jerusalem!
Riding on a donkey,
He's off to Jerusalem!

Shout, 'Hosanna!' everyone,
For we know he is God's Son.
Shout for King Jesus!
He's off to Jerusalem!

He's off to Jerusalem!
He's off to Jerusalem!
Riding on a donkey,
He's off to Jerusalem!

 Let's Join In! Scripture Union 1990 op

 Matthew 21:1–11; Mark 11:1–11; Luke 19:28–38; John 12:12–19

Even very young children will enjoy joining in the chorus. Pretend to be the people in the crowd and welcome Jesus, together.

Hosanna! Hooray!

Hosanna, hosanna, hosanna!
Hooray, hooray, hooray!
Jesus is riding a donkey.
King Jesus is coming this way!

 Sue Andrews

Matthew 21:1–11; Mark 11:1–11; Luke 19:28–38; John 12:12–19

Praise King Jesus

Thank you, Jesus,
Praise King Jesus.
We give you our love.
Praise King Jesus.
We sing your praise.
Praise King Jesus.
We follow your way.
Praise King Jesus.
Thank you for helping us.
Praise King Jesus.
Help us to remember –
Praise King Jesus.

 Bubbles for Leaders January–March 2005

Matthew 21:1–11; Mark 11:1–11; Luke 19:28–38; John 12:12–19

A meal with Jesus

Eat and remember

Jesus gave his friends some bread.
'Eat and remember me,' he said.
Jesus gave his friends some wine.
'Remember you are friends of mine.'

 Christine Orme

 Matthew 26:26–30; Mark 14:22–26; Luke 22:14–23;
1 Corinthians 11:23–25

Just like Jesus

Jesus showed us what to do,
What to do, what to do,
Jesus showed us what to do
So we can serve our friends.

He washed all the dirty feet,
Dirty feet, dirty feet,
He washed all the dirty feet
And dried them with a towel.

He wants us to serve our friends,
Serve our friends, serve our friends,
He wants us to serve our friends,
To show our love for God.

We will treat our friends just right,
Friends just right, friends just right.
We will treat our friends just right
To show our love for God.

 Ruth Dell

 John 13:1–20

 'Mary had a little lamb'

Remembering Jesus

It's Passover, it's Passover,
And Jesus tells his friends,
He's going to die and go away –
This good time's going to end.

It's Passover, it's Passover,
His friends are feeling sad,
But Jesus says he'll come alive
Again – then they'll be glad.

It's Passover, it's Passover,
See Jesus break the bread,
'This is my body, given for you,
Remember me,' he said.

It's Passover, it's Passover,
See Jesus take the wine,
'Remember, when you drink this
That you are friends of mine.'

And so today, and so today,
We think how Jesus died,
And how he came alive again,
And how his friends all cried.

We won't forget, we won't forget,
What Jesus said that day,
We'll eat the bread and drink the wine,
Remembering him this way.

 Christine Orme

 Matthew 26:17–30; Mark 14:12–21; Luke 22:7–13; John 13:21–30

Easter

Jesus is alive!

Here is the tomb where Jesus lay.
(Line up two fists.)
Here is the stone that rolled right away.
(Roll away one fist.)
A bright shining angel
(Wiggle fingers in an arc.)
Said, 'Come, look inside.
(Beckon with one finger.)
Your friend isn't dead.
(Wag one finger back and forth.)
Jesus is alive!'
(Throw hands up in joy.)

Here is Lord Jesus,
(Put out one hand.)
And here are his friends.
(Put out other hand.)
They hug Jesus' feet
(Clasp wrist with other hand.)
And shout out again,
'Jesus is alive!'
(Throw hands up in joy.)

 Mary Houlgate

 Matthew 28:1–15; Mark 16:1–8; Luke 24:1–12; John 20:1–10

Easter shout

Jesus died and all his friends were sad,
THEN…
Jesus came alive and all his friends were glad!

 Val Mullally

 Matthew 27:31 – 28:10; Mark 15:22 – 16:8; Luke 23:27 – 24:12; John 19:17 – 20:10

 A praise shout to celebrate Jesus' resurrection.

What do you see?

Mary, Mary, what do you see?
'I see an empty grave.
Where can Jesus be?'

Mary, Mary, what do you see?
'I see two angels.
Where can Jesus be?'

Mary, Mary, what do you see?
'I see a gardener.
Where can Jesus be?'

Mary, Mary, what do you see?
'I see Jesus!
He is here with me!'

 Priscilla Trood

 John 20:11–18; Mark 16:9–11

He's alive!

He's alive! He's alive!
Jesus died and rose again –
Now he's alive!

 From *Tiddlywinks: The Big Yellow Book*, Scripture Union 2003

 Mark 16:9–20; Matthew 28:9,10; John 20:11–18

 'Hot cross buns'

 Sing loudly and enthusiastically.

Easter

Roll the stone away

Roll, roll, roll the stone,
Roll the stone away!
Jesus is alive again,
Hip, hip, hip hooray!

 Mary Houlgate

 Matthew 28:1–15; Mark 16:1–8; Luke 24:1–12; John 20:1–10

 'Row, row, row your boat'

 Roll your hands over each other as you roll the stone away.

Clap your hands

Clap your hands, sing praise to Jesus,
He's alive! He's alive!
Clap your hands, sing praise to Jesus,
Shout, 'Hooray!' everyone.

Stamp your feet, sing praise to Jesus,
He's alive! He's alive!
Stamp your feet, sing praise to Jesus,
Shout, 'Hooray!' everyone.

Dance and jump, sing praise to Jesus,
He's alive! He's alive!
Dance and jump, sing praise to Jesus,
Shout, 'Hooray!' everyone.

(Quietly.)
Let's sit here and talk to Jesus,
He's alive! He's alive!
Let's sit here and talk to Jesus,
Talk to God, everyone.

 Bubbles for Leaders January–March 2005

 Luke 24:1–12; Matthew 28:1–10; Mark 16:1–8; John 20:1–10

 'Praise him, praise him all you little children'

 Clap, sing, shout, stamp, dance and jump to show how you feel about Jesus being alive! The last verse will help you calm the excitement.

Easter time

Thank you, God, for Easter time.
Thank you, God, for Easter time.
Thank you, Jesus, you're alive.
Thank you, Jesus, you're alive.
Thank you that we all can see –
Thank you that we all can see –
Jesus died for you and me.
Jesus died for you and me.
Lord, we thank you every day –
Lord, we thank you every day –
Jesus is alive always!
Jesus is alive always!

 Ali Matchett

 Mark 16:9–20; Matthew 28:9–20; John 20:11–23; Luke 24:13–53

 Lead the children in this prayer rhyme. Encourage them to repeat each phrase after you. Repeat this a couple of times to encourage the children to join in thanking God that Jesus is alive. You might like to add a clapped rhythm.

Easter

Easter prayer

Jesus,
(Point upwards.)
You love me.
(Point to yourself.)
I'm so happy
(Use your index finger to draw a big smile on your face.)
You are here.
You are alive today
(Jump up high.)
And I can shout,
(Put your hands to your mouth.)
'Thank you for Easter!'
(Shout!)

Jesus,
(Point upwards.)
You love us.
(Point to yourself.)
We're so happy
(Use your index finger to draw a big smile on your face.)
You are here.
You are alive today
(Jump up high.)
And we can shout,
(Put your hands to your mouth.)
'Thank you for Easter!'
(Shout!)

 Ali Matchett

 Mark 16:1–8; Matthew 28:1–8; Luke 24:1–12; John 20:1–10

 Practise the words and actions and then use these as a prayer.

Use this pattern to pray at other times. Adapt the prayer by changing the last line: you could add each child's name in turn or let the children suggest things they would like to say thank you for and put those in the prayer.

I will shout

I will shout with my mouth,
I will shout out loud!
'Cos Jesus is alive!
(Say a praise shout together: 'Jesus is alive! Jesus is alive! Jesus is alive! Hooray!')

I will dance with my feet,
I will dance and skip!
'Cos Jesus is alive!
(Play music and dance freely.)

I will sing with my voice,
I'll sing high and low!
'Cos Jesus is alive!
(Sing your group's favourite worship song.)

I will clap with my hands,
I will clap them hard!
'Cos Jesus is alive!
(Clap out a rhythm or clap to your chosen song.)

I will wave with my arms,
I will wave them high!
'Cos Jesus is alive!
(Wave happily.)

 Priscilla Trood

 Luke 24:36–49; Matthew 28:16–20; Mark 16:14–18; John 20:19–23; Acts 1:6–8

 Pause between each verse to experience other ways of worship.

Easter

Jesus is alive today!

Clap your hands and shout, 'Hooray!'
Jesus is alive today!

Stamp your feet and turn around,
Reach up high – and touch the ground,
Clap your hands and shout, 'Hooray!'
Jesus is alive today!

Touch your knees and touch your toes,
Touch your shoulders, touch your nose,
Stamp your feet and turn around,
Reach up high – and touch the ground,
Clap your hands and shout, 'Hooray!'
Jesus is alive today!

Dance around and skip about,
Praise God with a joyful shout!
Touch your knees and touch your toes,
Touch your shoulders, touch your nose,
Stamp your feet and turn around,
Reach up high – and touch the ground,
Clap your hands and shout, 'Hooray!'
Jesus is alive today!

 Priscilla Trood

 Luke 24:36–49; Matthew 28: 16–20; Mark 16:14–18; John 20:19–23; Acts 1:6–8

Sunday evening

It was Sunday evening and we'd locked the door.
Our dear friend, Jesus, wasn't with us any more.
The people who had killed him might come for us too.
We were all too frightened to know what to do.

Suddenly, we had a great surprise!
Jesus was right there! We rubbed our eyes!
But it wasn't a dream – he really was there!
All we wanted to do was stand and stare!

He said, 'Peace be with you. Don't be afraid.
Now, listen to the plans that God has made;
God wants you to tell people all about me.
The Holy Spirit will help you – just wait and see.'

He breathed gently on each of us, there in the room
'Receive the Spirit – he'll come to you soon.
He'll help you tell others all about me,
And he'll help you be kind, as God wants you to be.'

 Christine Orme

 John 20:19–23; Matthew 28:16–20; Mark 16:14–18; Luke 24:36–49

Easter

Fish are swimming

Fish are swimming, fish are swimming,
In the sea, in the sea,
Look at all the fishes, look at all the fishes,
In the sea, in the sea.
(Open and close fingers, to look like a fish's mouth.)

Men are coming, men are coming,
In their boat, in their boat,
Trying to catch the fishes, trying to catch the fishes,
In the sea, in the sea.
(Rock from side to side.)

Fish are hiding, fish are hiding,
In the sea, in the sea,
Now the men can't find them,
Now the men can't find them,
In the sea, in the sea.
(Put hands together and wiggle them, like fish swimming.)

Going home now, going home now,
Very sad, very sad,
They could find no fishes, they could find no fishes,
In the sea, in the sea.
(Rock side to side.)

Here comes Jesus, here comes Jesus,
By the sea, by the sea,
'Have you caught some fishes? Have you caught some fishes?'
'No,' they say. 'No,' they say.
(Rock side to side.)

'Put your net out, put your net out.
Pull it in, pull it in.'
The net is full of fishes! The net is full of fishes!
From the sea, from the sea!
(Mime throwing net out – and trying to haul it back in.)

Jesus helped them, Jesus helped them,
They were glad, they were glad.
Then they went for breakfast, then they went for breakfast,
By the sea, by the sea.

 Adapted from *Sing, Say and Move*, Scripture Union 1981 op

 John 21:1–14

 'Frère Jacques'

Remember he's alive

Clap your hands for Jesus!
Clap your hands for Jesus!
Clap your hands for Jesus!
Remember he's alive!

 Sheila Clift

 Luke 24:36–49; Matthew 28:16–20; Mark 16:14–18; John 20:19–23; Acts 1:6–8

 Clap along to this praise shout.

Close to God

Tell your friends

Tell your friends about me,
Everywhere you go.
Tell them all the things I did,
Everything you know!

Tell your friends I love them.
(And I love you, too!)
Tell your friends I'll always be
With them (and with you)!

Tell your friends I want to
Help them every day.
Tell your friends this good news
So they choose the Jesus way!

 Christine Orme

 Matthew 28:16–20; Mark 16:14–18; Luke 24:36–49;
John 20:19–23; Acts 1:6–8

 Explain that these words are like the ones Jesus said to his friends,
just before he went back to heaven.

God is with us

Loving God, you are with us all the time.
You are with us all the time.
You are with us when we are sad,
You are with us all the time.
You are with us when we are cross,
You are with us all the time.
You are with us when we are lonely,
You are with us all the time.
You are with us when we are ill or hurt,
You are with us all the time.
You are with us when we are happy and excited,
You are with us all the time.

And we want to say a great big 'Thank you!'
Thank you!

 Christine Wright

 Acts 16:11–15; Leviticus 26:12; Deuteronomy 31:8; Joshua 1:5;
Psalm 27; Isaiah 33:6

God is here

Thank you, God, you're always here,
Thank you, God, you're always here,
Thank you, God, you're always here,
You're always close to me.

You are with me when I'm feeling *glad,*
You are with me when I'm feeling *glad,*
You are with me when I'm feeling *glad,*
You're always close to me.

 Ali Matchett

 Joshua 1:1–9

 'Thank you, Lord, for this fine day'

 Create more verses about how you feel (… when I'm feeling sad/
cross/tired…) and then about things we do or places we go. Try
one or two of these (…when I run and jump… when I go to
church) and encourage the children to suggest other ideas. If the
children are enjoying the song, see how long you can make it!

The Holy Spirit

Do not worry!

Jesus told us not to worry
When he goes away.
He will send another friend
To be with us each day.

'Do not worry, do not worry,'
He told us that night.
'When I go, don't be afraid,
When I leave your sight.'

'I will send another helper,
When I go away.
You will have God's Holy Spirit
With you every day.'

 SALT 3 to 4+ April–June 2004

 John 14

He helps us

Give thanks to God for he is good!
God's Holy Spirit helps us!
God sent Jesus to show us what God is like.
God's Holy Spirit helps us!
God takes care of us every day.
God's Holy Spirit helps us!
God looks after us when we're asleep.
God's Holy Spirit helps us!
God knows everything we need.
God's Holy Spirit helps us!
When we don't know what to do,
God's Holy Spirit helps us!
When we are afraid,
God's Holy Spirit helps us!
When we find it hard to obey,
God's Holy Spirit helps us!
Give thanks to God for he is good!
God's Holy Spirit helps us!

 Christine Orme

 John 20:19–23; Matthew 28:16–20; Mark 16:14–18;
Luke 24:36–49

Jesus promised

Jesus promised, Jesus promised,
To send a helper, to send a helper.
Thank you, Jesus, thank you, Jesus,
For your promise, for your promise.

Jesus promised, Jesus promised,
That he loves us, that he loves us.
Thank you, Jesus, thank you, Jesus,
For your promise, for your promise.

 Ali Matchett

 Acts 2:1–14

 'London's burning'

 Encourage them to help you make up verses to thank Jesus for
keeping his promises. Adapt the second line as you continue the
song.

Holy Spirit Day

God's Holy Spirit

Mummies and daddies and brothers and sisters,
These are the people God sends.
People who're ready to help us,
Doctors and teachers and friends.

Grannies and grandads and aunties and uncles,
Posties and shopkeepers too.
How would we manage without them?
How would we know what to do?

But the best helper's God's Holy Spirit,
We can't see him or touch him or hear,
But he's always beside us, ready to help us,
We're glad that he's always so near.

 SALT 3 to 4+ April–June 2004

 John 14

Holy Spirit Day

Jesus promised a helper would come,
Helper would come, helper would come.
Jesus promised a helper would come,
On Holy Spirit Day.

The sound of a wind came filling the room,
Filling the room, filling the room.
The sound of a wind came filling the room,
On Holy Spirit Day.

A special fire touched on all their heads,
All their heads, all their heads.
A special fire touched on all their heads,
On Holy Spirit Day.

They ran out to talk of Jesus' love,
Jesus' love, Jesus' love.
They ran out to talk of Jesus' love,
On Holy Spirit Day.

The Holy Spirit has come to stay,
Come to stay, come to stay.
The Holy Spirit has come to stay,
On Holy Spirit Day.

 Ali Matchett

 Acts 2:1–14

 'Here we go round the mulberry bush'

 If you prefer, change the last line of each verse to: 'He came at Pentecost'.

Holy Spirit Day

Jesus is with us

Jesus is with us,
He's promised to be.
Jesus is with us,
He loves you and me.
Jesus is with us,
In good times and bad.
Jesus is with us –
I'm very glad!

 SALT 3 to 4+ April–June 2003

 Acts 2:1–14

 Say loudly as a praise shout and declaration; or quietly as a thoughtful prayer.

God sends the Holy Spirit

Jesus'friends were sad and frightened
When he went away,
Back to heaven to his **Father**,
'Wait,' he said,'and pray.
God will send his **Holy Spirit** –
He'll help you each day.'

They heard a big wind rushing, then
Saw fire on every head!
God had sent the **Holy Spirit**
Just as **Jesus** said.
Now they felt – not sad and frightened –
But glad and safe instead!

 SALT 3 to 4+ April–June 2002

 Acts 2

 Divide the children into three groups: Father, Jesus and Holy Spirit. When 'their' name is mentioned in the rhyme, the children should jump up, then sit down again. When the name *God* is mentioned, they should all jump up.

Father, Son and Holy Spirit

One is God the Father who made the world.
Two is his Son, Jesus, who died on the cross.
Three is the Holy Spirit sent to help us,
One, two, three, this is our God.

One is God the Father who loves us so much.
Two is his Son, Jesus, who rose from the dead.
Three is the Holy Spirit always with us,
One, two, three, this is our God.

 Kathleen Crawford

 Acts 2:22–47

 Touch the thumb for one, index finger for two, and middle finger for three.

The early church

Philip's story

Here is the desert, sandy and dry,
Where usually nobody ever goes by,
And where nobody ever would really have guessed,
That God would show that he always knows best.

Here is Philip, standing right by the way,
('Walk' Philip on to the desert.)
Sent by an angel on that very day,
Into the desert, sandy and dry,
Where usually nobody ever goes by,
And where nobody ever would really have guessed,
That God would show that he always knows best.

Here's an important man riding by,
(Bring the chariot and man from the opposite side,
getting closer to Philip.)
Reading a book in his chariot high,
Coming to Philip, standing right by the way,
Sent by an angel on that very day,
Into the desert, sandy and dry,
Where usually nobody ever goes by,
And where nobody ever would really have guessed,
That God would show that he always knows best.

Here are the difficult words in the book,
That the man puzzled over as he took a look,
That very important man riding by,
Reading the book in his chariot high,
Coming to Philip, standing right by the way,
(Stop the chariot by Philip.)
Sent by an angel on that very day,
Into the desert, sandy and dry,
Where usually nobody ever goes by,
And where nobody ever would really have guessed,
That God would show that he always knows best.

The book's about Jesus, and Philip began,
(Put Philip in the chariot too.)
To explain to the very important man,
All of the difficult words in the book,
That the man puzzled over as he took a look,
That very important man riding by,
Reading the book in his chariot high,
Coming to Philip, standing right by the way,
Sent by an angel on that very day,
Into the desert, sandy and dry,

Where usually nobody ever goes by,
And where nobody ever would really have guessed,
That God would show that he always knows best.

The important man listened as hard as he could,
And learnt about Jesus, so kind and so good,
And when Philip finished, the man at the end
Said, 'I'd like to have Jesus now as my friend.'
So that day in the desert the two men were blessed,
Because God showed them both that he always
knows best.

 Marjory Francis

 Acts 8:26–40

 Use dolls or puppets and a box as a chariot to act out the events of this story.

The early church

Dorcas

Dorcas made clothes for poor people.
Dorcas was such a good friend.
When Dorcas was sick, everybody was sad.
And then her life came to an end.

Peter came rushing from Lydda.
He asked Jesus what he should do.
'Get up now, Dorcas!' said Peter.
She came back to life – good as new!

 Christine Orme

 Acts 9:36–43

 Dramatise the rhyme by miming the roles of Dorcas or Peter.

Barnabas

Barnabas, Barnabas, where are you going?
A long way from home; over the sea.
I'm going to Jerusalem.
And God's with me!

Barnabas, Barnabas, where are you going?
I'm meeting the church to help them see
That Paul is a Christian.
And God's with me!

Barnabas, Barnabas, where are you going?
All round the world by land and sea
To talk about Jesus.
And God's with me!

 Christine Wright

 Acts 4:36,37; 9:26–30; 13:1–5

Agabus' message

Tell me a story Agabus.
What do you know?
(Point to head.)
What do you see?
(Point to eyes.)
Tell me a story Agabus.
Has God got a message for me?
(Point upwards and then to self.)

'A famine will come,' said Agabus.
'That's what I know,
(Point to head.)
That's what I see.
(Point to eyes.)
A famine will come,' said Agabus,
'And Christians will be hungry.'
(Rub tummy.)

We care very much Agabus,
That's what we know,
(Point to head.)
That's what we'll see,
(Point to eyes.)
We care very much, Agabus,
We'll make sure they have food for tea!
(Pretend to eat and smile!)

 Elizabeth Whitworth

 Acts 11:27–30

The early church

Cornelius and Peter

One Roman gentleman,
(Show one finger.)
Cornelius is his name,
Loves God,
(Hands on heart.)
And prays to him every day.
(Hands together.)

One Roman gentleman,
Cornelius is his name,
Loves God,
And wants to hear what God says.
(Hand cupped to ear.)

One Roman gentleman,
Cornelius is his name,
Asks for Peter,
To come to talk to him.
(Beckon.)

Peter tells Cornelius,
(Wag finger.)
'Jesus loves us all.'
(Point upwards; then hands over heart; then reaching out to all.)
Cornelius is happy
Because Jesus is his friend.

 Val Mullally

 Acts 10

Peter in prison

Peter, in prison, was fast asleep,
(Pretend to be asleep.)
Fast asleep, fast asleep,
Peter, in prison, was fast asleep,
And God was with him, there.

Peter's friends were praying for him,
(Pretend to pray.)
Praying for him, praying for him,
Peter's friends were praying for him,
And God was with him, there.

An angel came and set him free,
Set him free, set him free,
(Shake hands and feet, as chains fall off!)
An angel came and set him free,
And God was with him, there.

Peter walked to Mary's house,
(Walk on the spot.)
Mary's house, Mary's house,
Peter walked to Mary's house,
And God was with him, there.

Everyone is praising God,
(Wave arms in the air, to praise God.)
Praising God, praising God,
Everyone is praising God,
And God is with us here.

God is looking after us,
(All hold hands in a circle.)
After us, after us,
God is looking after us,
And God is with us here.

 Christine Wright

 Acts 12:4–17

 'Here we go round the Mulberry bush'

Paul

On the road

Paul's feet on the road went plod, plod, plod,
(March slowly on the spot.)
Plod, plod, plod, plod, plod, plod,
Paul's feet on the road went plod, plod, plod,
On the road.

Paul saw a bright light up in the sky,
(Shield eyes from the light.)
Up in the sky, up in the sky,
Paul saw a bright light up in the sky,
On the road.

Paul heard Jesus speak to him,
(Beckon.)
Speak to him, speak to him,
Paul heard Jesus speak to him,
On the road.

When Paul stood up, he could not see,
(Cover eyes with hands.)
Could not see, could not see,
When Paul stood up, he could not see,
On the road.

But Ananias prayed for him,
(Hands together.)
Prayed for him, prayed for him,
But Ananias prayed for him,
In the house.

Paul opened his eyes – now he could see,
(Open eyes and look around.)
He could see, he could see,
Paul opened his eyes – now he could see,
In the house.

Now Paul was part of God's family,
(All hold hands in a circle.)
Family, family,
Now Paul was part of God's family,
Everywhere!

SALT 3 to 4+ January–March 2004

Acts 9:1–25

'The wheels on the bus'

For a shorter version, sing the first three and last verses.

Lydia

Lydia knows that God is with her.
(Hug yourself.)
With her day and night.
(Hands over eyes, then take them away.)
When she needs God, God is with her.
(Hug yourself.)
She will be all right.
(Thumbs up.)

Christine Wright

Acts 16:11–15

Talk about times when the children might need to know that God is there – when they are ill, sad or upset. Assure the children that whenever they need God, he is there. Say the rhyme again, changing the name 'Lydia' to each of the children's names in turn: *Connor* knows that God is with *him*, With *him* day and night. When *he* needs God, God is with *him*. *He* will be all right.

Paul

Down by the riverside

Paul and Silas went walking,
Down by the riverside,
Down by the riverside,
In the town of Philippi.
Paul and Silas went walking,
Down by the riverside,
Down by the riverside.

Paul and Silas got talking,
Down by the riverside,
Down by the riverside,
In the town of Philippi.
Paul and Silas got talking,
Down by the riverside,
Down by the riverside.

They talked about Jesus,
Down by the riverside,
Down by the riverside,
In the town of Philippi.
They talked about Jesus,
Down by the riverside,
Down by the riverside.

The women all listened,
Down by the riverside,
Down by the riverside,
In the town of Philippi.
The women all listened,
Down by the riverside,
Down by the riverside.

A woman called Lydia,
Believed in Jesus,
Down by the riverside,
In the town of Philippi.
A woman called Lydia
Believed in Jesus,
Down by the riverside.

So a new church was started,
Down by the riverside,
Down by the riverside,
In the town of Philippi.
So a new church was started,
Down by the riverside,
Down by the riverside.

 Christine Orme

 Acts 16:11–15

 'Gonna lay down my burden'

Prison walls

Prison walls are falling down,
Falling down, falling down,
Prison walls are falling down,
Praise to Jesus!

Chains are falling off our hands,
Off our hands, off our hands,
Chains are falling off our hands,
Praise to Jesus!

Window bars are falling down,
Falling down, falling down,
Window bars are falling down,
Praise to Jesus!

 Maggie Barfield

 Acts 16:25–28

 'London Bridge is falling down'

 Have fun, falling down in each verse and then jumping up to praise Jesus.

Paul

Paul and Silas

Paul and Silas sit in the cold dark prison.
Their backs are very sore but the other prisoners listen
To Paul and Silas singing songs of praise,
They belong to Jesus so they pray to him always.

Paul and Silas feel the prison start to shake.
Then all their chains fall off in the great earthquake.
Paul and Silas see the jailer full of fear.
'Don't worry!' shouts Paul. 'We're all still here!'

Paul and Silas tell the jailer what to do:
'Believe in Jesus right away and you'll belong too!'

 Christine Orme

 Acts 16:25–34

 Ask the children what they think happened next. What did the jailer say? He and all his family became friends of Jesus!

Apollos

Here is Apollos,
(Hold up index finger.)
A very clever man.
(Tap forehead.)
Can he read and write well?
Yes, he can.
(Nod.)
But he's not too proud to learn more!

Here is Apollos,
Preaching to a crowd,
(Hold up and wave fingers of other hand.)
Talking about Jesus,
Right out loud!
But he's not too proud to learn more!

Here is Apollos,
Not talking at all.
Listening gladly,
To friends of Paul,
Because he's not too proud to learn more!

 Let's Join In! Scripture Union 1990 op

 Acts 18:24–28

A letter to Timothy

Hello Tim. This is Paul,
Don't be scared. God helps us all.
Wish I could be with you.
I just want to tell you –
Read the Bible; follow in God's way.

 Alison Dayer

 2 Timothy 1:3–10; 3:14–17

 'Postman Pat'

 Paul wrote this to his young friend Timothy but his advice is good for all of us!

Paul

Don't go, Paul!

Don't go, Paul! Don't go, Paul!
Don't go to Jerusalem!
Don't go, Paul! Don't go, Paul!
Please don't go!

I will go! I will go!
God wants me to go to Jerusalem!
I will go! I will go!
I will do what God tells me to do.

Don't go, Paul! Don't go, Paul!
You won't be safe in Jerusalem!
Don't go, Paul! Don't go, Paul!
Please don't go!

I will go! I will go!
God wants me to go to Jerusalem!
I will go! I will go!
I will do what God tells me to do.

Don't go, Paul! Don't go, Paul!
They'll lock you up in Jerusalem!
Don't go, Paul! Don't go, Paul!
Please don't go!

I will go! I will go!
God wants me to go to Jerusalem!
I will go! I will go!
I will do what God tells me to do.

SALT 3 to 4+ January–March 2004

Acts 21:1–16

Explain that Paul's friends did not want him to go to Jerusalem because they did not want him to be in danger or trouble. But Paul knew God still wanted him to go – so he did. Use the final line as a prayer and promise to God.

Safe in the storm

Safe in the storm,
Safe in the storm,
God, keep the travellers
Safe in the storm.

Safe in the storm,
Safe in the storm,
God kept the travellers
Safe in the storm.

Safe where they are,
Safe where they are,
God, keep your people
Safe where they are.

Safe where they are,
Safe where they are,
God keeps his people
Safe where they are.

Safe where we are,
Safe where we are,
God, keep us and our friends
Safe where we are.

Safe where we are,
Safe where we are,
God keeps us and our friends
Safe where we are.

Christine Wright

Acts 27

Say alternate verses as a request-and-response. The first verse of each pair asks God to keep people safe; the second verse confirms that he does do so.

A dream of heaven

John's dream

My name's John! I've seen Jesus!
God has shown me in a dream.
Jesus was shining! Eyes like firelight,
Face like sunshine, his hands held stars!

His feet were strong, like bright, clean metal.
His hair was soft, like warm, pure wool.
I felt frightened of his great brilliance,
But Jesus touched me and calmed my fear.

He said, 'Listen, I am mighty,
But I love you, I'll always care.'
My name's John. I've seen Jesus!
He's so wonderful! Thank you God.

 Mary Houlgate

 Matthew 24:3, 29–51; Revelation 1

Bright love

Be near us, Lord Jesus, your love is so bright,
You make sad people happy and dark places light.
Help us shine with love like you.

 Mary Houlgate

 Matthew 24:3, 29–51; Revelation 1

All day long

The people on earth, they all praise God,
All praise God, all praise God,
The people on earth, they all praise God,
All day long.

The angels in heaven worship God,
Worship God, worship God,
The angels in heaven worship God,
All day long.

The grown-ups and the children pray to God,
Pray to God, pray to God,
The grown-ups and the children pray to God,
All day long.

The children and the grown-ups sing to God,
Sing to God, sing to God,
The children and the grown-ups sing to God,
All day long.

The people on earth, they all praise God,
All praise God, all praise God,
The people on earth, they all praise God,
All day long.

 SALT 3 to 4+ April–June 2003

 Revelation 7:9–17

 'The wheels on the bus'

Index

Have you enjoyed this book?

Then take a look at the Big Books in the *Tiddlywinks* range. Why not try them all?